I0824923

PARY BABAN
PHOTOGRAPHY BY CLARE WINFIELD

NANDÊN

RECIPES FROM MY KURDISH KITCHEN

rps
RYLAND PETERS & SMALL

To my hometown, Qaladze, and my land, Kurdistan.
To all the women who have inspired me – my mum, grandmother and my beloved aunties that helped me get to where I am today.
To my sons and husband, who walked the journey with me.

Senior Designer Megan Smith
Senior Editor Abi Waters
Editorial Director Julia Charles
Production Director Patricia Harrington
Creative Director Leslie Harrington
Food Stylist Kathy Kordalis
Prop Stylist Rosie Jenkins
Indexer Vanessa Bird

First published in 2026 by
Ryland Peters & Small
20–21 Jockey's Fields,
London WC1R 4BW
and
1452 Davis Bugg Road
Warrenton, NC 27589

www.rylandpeters.com
email: euregulations@rylandpeters.com

10 9 8 7 6 5 4 3 2 1

Printed in China.

ISBN: 978-1-78879-746-7

A CIP record for this book is available from the British Library. US Library of Congress cataloging-in-Publication Data has been applied for.

The authorised representative in the EEA is
Authorised Rep Compliance Ltd.,
Ground Floor, 71 Lower Baggot Street,
Dublin, D02 P593, Ireland
www.arccompliance.com

NOTES

- Both metric and imperial measurements are used in the recipes. Follow one set of measurements throughout as they are not necessarily interchangeable.
- All spoon measurements are level, unless specified otherwise.
5 ml = 1 teaspoon
15 ml = 1 tablespoon
- Ovens should be preheated to the specified temperature.
- Butter is always unsalted, unless specified otherwise.
- Eggs are always UK large/US extra-large.
- Herbs are always fresh, unless specified otherwise.
- All vegetables are peeled, unless specified otherwise.
- When a recipe calls for the grated zest of citrus fruit, use unwaxed fruit and wash well before using.
- Uncooked or partially cooked eggs should not be served to the very old, frail, young children, pregnant women or those with compromised immune systems.

Contents

Introduction

Kurdistan itself is not a recognized nation-state, but we are a people with a strong cultural identity. Despite generations of political hardship, displacement and the erasure of our heritage, our language, music and cuisine continue to thrive. That resilience is reflected in our food. It is fresh, simple, generous, meant to be shared and comes with a deep connection to the land; we use our intuition to tap into the land's resourcefulness to produce a natural, yet delicious cuisine. The variety in the terrain allows for a diversity in the foods and cooking styles. As we say: 'We have no friends but the mountains'. This saying speaks not only to our political isolation, but to the profound and enduring relationship we have with our land.

My home, my land

I was born in Qaladze, in southern Kurdistan, a place with a rich history of resistance and community. Qaladze is located in the middle of Pishdar District, north of Slemani province in Bashur, and is surrounded by mountains. I grew up within a big family with 11 siblings in total (I am the fifth child). My family kept livestock and produced our own milk, cheese, yogurts and *ron-i-xolati* (clarified butter). We also grew and processed our own grains and pulses.

Our lifestyle was semi-nomadic; during the summer months, we would farm and harvest in the plains and in the winter we would dry and cure the summer produce, storing it to see us through the colder months. Our home was located quite close to the Qalat mound, where we spent many winters sledging down the snow-covered hill in cardboard boxes. Qaladze (Qala duzê – *Qala* meaning 'mound', *duzê* means 'two rivers' so 'the mound between two rivers') is often referred to as Namrê, which means 'never dies' because of its resilient spirit.

We were three generations all living in the same house which had an indoor kitchen, an outdoor kitchen and a courtyard. The outdoor kitchen in the yard was a typical Kurdish house made out of mud and straw. There were cupboards full of grains, flour and a big barrel of bread kept in a cool place. In the middle of this space there was a large fire pit, around which our grandmother would place three big stones in order to be able to cook over the wood fire. Early in the morning she would milk our cow and warm the fresh milk over the open fire as my siblings and I all sat with her. She would then put some bread in a bowl and ladle milk over the top, adding just a tiny bit of sugar before handing it to each of us to eat. She had about seven kittens that she would also give bread and milk to and a cupboard called a *kûlana* where she would put them (or her chickens) if it was especially cold weather and to protect them from any predators (foxes, wild dogs and other animals).

Life then was simple with lots of love and support from our community, both in the good times and during the struggles. When someone was getting married, the celebration would go on for three days and when someone died we would all come together to help cook at their home and be there for the family.

Nandên is the Kurdish word for 'kitchen' (and also sometimes spelled or pronounced 'nandine'). The kitchen has always been the centre of our home, where most of my memories were born: cooking, eating and sharing stories with my family and friends. In Kurdish communities, food is a symbol of the most important aspects of our culture: tradition, hospitality and respect, kinship and connection. I wanted to extend that welcome in my restaurant, whilst also celebrating the culinary traditions of my heritage. It has been amazing to connect with people from so many different cultures and see them enjoy my food and discover dishes and flavours that they have never tried before.

Qazwan Kurdish Coffee
Wild Dried Shallots
7SPICE
Qazwan Salad Dressing
Amba
Nuts

My journey

The genocide and mass destruction by Saddam Hussein's government between 1986–1989 meant that my home town of Qaladze was destroyed in 1989. He demolished more than 250 villages and forced 100,000 residents to leave the town and move to camps as part of the Anfal genocide against the Kurds. In 1988, I left Qaladze as the campaign began. Just one month before, Halabja was chemically bombed, and by 1989 Qaladze was demolished, even putting cement in the springs and streams to stop any life in the area. Many residents fled to camps that were overcrowded with limited resources, risking malnutrition and many other complications.

My family and I were one of many who decided instead to make the perilous journey to the mountains to escape. It took us nine days and nights to reach the border of east Kurdistan. The only things we took with us were warm clothes, some folded flat bread, cured meats and dried fruits. At the time I was just 18 years old. We made our way through the Qandil mountain to Gwêzê village on the border, walking through the night and hiding when the sun rose. My dad's side of the family were living in east Kurdistan at the time and they took us to Bewran village between Qaladze and Sardasht town. We went through Shin-wê, Nalas, Dukanan villages, staying with relatives along the way. They were all farmers and shepherds, foraging and making cheese using traditional techniques. I found myself becoming interested in foraging, fermenting and curing, and questioned our relatives endlessly about how they sourced and cooked their food, what ingredients they used, and wrote it all down in a notebook. At the time of the genocide of the Kurdish people, I felt it was very important to document these traditions and keep a record of our unique history and culture as our people were threatened with eradication, and continue to be persecuted to this day. After the destruction of our town, many of the people returned to try and rebuild their homes and lives. The town was culturally progressive, it was a centrepoint for political discourse, cultural elevation and historically rich in poets, musicians and the resistance too. My family moved from east Kurdistan to South East London, where I still live today.

Our new life

In 1995 we arrived in the UK from east Kurdistan. My husband and I both worked in a newsagents, in Elephant & Castle in South East London. I went to college to take English language classes and also completed a hairdressing and beauty therapy course, in between taking the kids to school and working shifts at the newsagent kiosk. Our love and need for a local community was so entrenched in us from childhood, that we sought to find this type of connection in our new life. We helped out within the community, especially the older people, by delivering newspapers, milk and bread to them.

Alongside the papers and groceries we sold ready-made sandwiches. I wasn't too fond of them so I decided to make my own at home, researching popular sandwich fillings, such as coronation chicken, tuna and sweetcorn, and cheese and spring onion/scallion (using five different cheeses in my version!). After a while I started to experiment with the Kurdish flavours and ingredients that were more familiar to me, such as egg and sumac with red onion, and *Silqi surkrawa* (see page 95) and people loved it! Our next step was to take over the empty space next to the kiosk and become the Newsweek Sandwich Bar, now selling home-cooked Kurdish food alongside my existing offerings. I made kubba sandwiches, yaprax and shifta wraps, and larger portions of these fillings to be eaten as a meal. I made kebab/kabob at home every week and took it into the shop, adding it to wraps, serving it with rice, topping it with sumac. I also took *Kalana* (see page 151) in with me to sell, warming it up on a big pan on a small gas cooker, rolling it up and putting butter on it to serve. I soon had regular customers, mostly local people and office workers. They would pull up at the shop in their cars and order food to take with them as they headed into the city. Even bus drivers changing shifts, or waiting just a few minutes to regulate the service, would call out to me with their orders and by the time they approached the traffic lights, I would have their order ready and run out to hand it to them through the window.

The best part was the hustle and bustle of these mornings, everyone heading out for their day, people saying good morning to each other. I started to really get to know the local community and feel a part of it, forming good relationships. There was one customer in particular, Charlie, his wife had passed away, so I would make food for him to take home and he would buy us presents at Christmas. There were inevitably some instances of discrimination and racist behaviour but the positives far outweighed the negatives.

Growing our business

In 2011–2012 we changed the name of the Newsweek Sandwich Bar to Baban Café but I still needed more space to cook so we started looking for a bricks and mortar site and found what we wanted in Camberwell. We were warned against the quiet location in Vestry Road where many previous businesses had failed, and a neighbouring business started a petition against us setting up our café, but we persisted. Added to that, fellow Kurdish chefs said we were brave to put 'Kurdish food' on our signage as it would be unfamiliar to so many people. One chef warned me that he had opened his own Kurdish restaurant in North London but closed after just six months. I told him: 'If I don't do it, and you don't do it, then who will do it and when will we put our food on the map?' I was determined to represent Kurdish food and highlight our unique culinary traditions and not label it as something else.

On our first day of trading we made just £17, but this was still a success in my eyes. We couldn't have made it without the support of our local customers during those years and some of our 'day-one' customers who have since moved out of the area still come back to see us now. We opened a second branch in Camberwell Church Street in July 2019 and it was there we started getting noticed by food journalists including Jay Rayner, Jimi Famurewa, Helen Graves, Jonathan Nunn, and publications such as *Munchies, Vice, Eater, Time Out, The Guardian, Evening Standard, The Independent* and *The Peckham Peculiar*. We have since hosted supper clubs, parties, wedding celebrations, and in 2024 a Taste Cadets collaboration for Kurdish New Year. These days, as well as running the restaurant I work with Copleston Community Centre in Peckham, running 'Food on a Budget' classes, teaching Kurdish cooking and providing restaurant-grade lunches for a low cost.

I am so grateful to have fulfilled my dream of sharing the beauty of my Kurdish heritage with our new-found community and to have created such a beautiful space to call my own in my adopted home.

What is Kurdish cuisine?

Kurdish cuisine has such a simplicity to it, using spices in moderation to enhance the natural flavours of the ingredients we use. The focus is on fresh food, nourishment and delicious flavourings. Our way of eating has a deep and historic connection to the land, reflecting the fertile geography, semi-nomadic traditions and self-sufficient agricultural practices of our people. This profound link to the region known as Kurdistan, has shaped our unique culinary traditions for millennia.

There is a strong culture of animal herding in Kurdish life and this heavily influences our food. Shepherds guide their animals across biodiverse landscapes and there is often an opportunity to gather wild herbs, nuts, seeds, fruits and vegetables. This foraged and gathered fresh produce from the mountains and valleys is seasonal so how the land itself moves through the year dictates what we eat and the dishes we make. In springtime they will pick herbs such as wild garlic, oregano, *mandê/mandok* (see page 13), and rhubarb is a celebrated ingredient often sprinkled with salt and enjoyed as a snack.

Many of our traditional culinary techniques come from this need to work in harmony with nature and to be as resourceful as possible. Fermenting and drying are important ways of preserving food. Take *pêsta*, for example: a vessel made from cured animal skins that is used to store cheese in the ground or in caves and preserved in winter. Or *hyza*, a vessel made from animal skin used to store butter, or *kunda*, which is used to cool water and *dow* (yogurt drink) during the hotter months. We have trees such as the *dara ben* (mastik tree), which bears *qazwan*. People cut into the trunk and use mud cups to collect the sap/resin, which is then used to produce chewing gum and medicines.

Lamb and mutton are very popular meats in Kurdish cooking, although chicken is also eaten, and in winter geese and turkey are enjoyed. *Mreeshk kurdi* is the term we use to describe animals that are kept in an organic, free-range setting. When the animals are slaughtered, the meat is slow-cooked in its own fat, water and salt for a long time, or over hot charcoal. The charcoaled meat is then wrapped in *Nani tiri* (see page 146) to soak up the fat from the meat and soften the bread (this is called *nana chawra*).

Bread is a staple, if you don't have bread in your home, you don't have any food. One standout bread is nani tiri because of its versatility, it can be eaten with any dish, savoury, sour or sweet. Sometimes we would put soft figs or watermelon in rehydrated nani tiri and wrap it up to eat as a snack.

Kalana (see page 151) is another important bread as it is a very old bread, traditionally made to mark the beginning of spring. This is usually stuffed with the first batch of spring onions/scallions but before that we use wild garlic or one of our homemade cheeses (this was popular with shepherds in particular).

I use some ingredients in my kitchen that are key in Kurdish cooking. The main ones are kardu, kinger and qazwan. These are all very versatile and incredibly delicious - see the pages that follow for more information on these.

Kurdish ingredients

KARDU (LORDS-AND-LADIES)

Kardu is a type of vegetable. It cannot be eaten raw and must be cured thoroughly using sumac or lemon juice and olive oil for 2 hours or more (see page 134 for how to cure). You can sun-dry it or freeze to use at a later date. Its taste and texture is similar to spinach and can often be found in stews and stir fries. We make a stew and cook kardu with meat and tahini (Dahok province/Badinan) or cook it in the sauce made for dumplings, but where I'm from in Pishdar District and Rojhelat we cook it with rice (Qibuli kardu), then we stir-fry it with egg and onion and call it *Kardu surkrawa*. We make *Kardu ganm* as a soup in the winter months (see page 56). *Kardu rash*, when boiled and allowed to cool, is eaten as a mezze.

Alternatives: Spinach or Swiss chard can work for the texture, though the flavour is more subtle.

KINGER (WILD ARTICHOKE ROOT)

Kinger (also known as *gundeela*) is a prized spring vegetable with a flavour somewhere between wild artichoke and white asparagus, though its texture is more like the latter. It is the white part of the root of the vegetable and it can be pickled, fried or turned into stews like *Shley kinger* (with rhubarb and meat). Or simply sautéed with onion and butter; *Kinger surkrawa* is then topped with yogurt and browned butter for *Kinger û mast*.

After living in the UK for a while I found myself missing kinger so much – you couldn't find it in any shops, and postage from Kurdistan was too expensive. I found white asparagus and baby leek and prepared them in the same way as I would kinger and made *baboula* (a wrap). I seasoned the wrap with some sumac and gave one to my husband, saying that it was kinger. He asked in shock where I got it from and I said I got it from my sister. Then I made the same for my sister and she asked me the same question, where did you get this from with the same shock! I said my husband's family gave it to me. They both said it was delicious and couldn't tell the difference! When I told them that it was actually baby leek and white asparagus and they couldn't believe it.

Alternatives: White asparagus, baby leek (white part, similar flavour) or wild artichoke.

QAZWAN (PISTACIA ATLANTICA)

Qazwan comes from the *dara ben* (mastic tree) grown all over Kurdistan. The fresh berries are called qazwan. In spring they are soft and fresh, perfect for pickling, or using in salads or eaten as a snack. When pickled they are also really great to keep for the winter (using just salt and vinegar to preserve them).

As the shell becomes a bit harder but the flesh is soft, you can roast it and use it to make a hot drink much like coffee, only the flavour is earthy and nutty, similar to the pistachio. When the shell has completely hardened it is used to make prayer beads and bracelets.

Alternatives: Pickled qazwan can be substituted with capers for a similar salty-sour taste.

MANDÊ (MANDOK)

A rooted leafy vegetable similar to a carrot but tastes like kinger. It is mostly used for making Kurdish cheese, called *zhazhi* (see page 129).

GULWAN (GLWAN)

This is a type of nut tree similar to walnut and oak. The fruit hardens while it's left on the tree until late autumn and the inside becomes a powder used for curing animal skin to make leather. *Meshka* is a container made from cured lamb skin that is used to make our fermented yogurt drink (*Dow*, see page 160), *hyza* is used to keep butter, *kunda (kuna)* is used to store water cold, *pêsta* is used to store cheese called *paniri pêsta* (but the skin used for this container would have the wool left on it).

SUMAC (TIRSH)

This spice is an important ingredient in Kurdish cuisine. It is geographically specific and varies from region to region. In the Pishdar region, it grows yellow and sour, while in Badinan, it's a rich burgundy colour. The berries have little aroma, but a pleasing sour-fruit flavour. They are used whole or ground and can also be cracked, then soaked for 15–20 minutes in water and squeezed to release their astringent juice, which can be added to stews, yaprax and meat dishes. Ground sumac can be used in salad dressings, sprinkled on kebabs/kabobs or used to season fish and chicken.

SAFFLOWER (KAGHLY)

Safflowers were one of the most beautiful parts of my childhood. Every summer in a small village near Qaladze, farmers would scatter safflower seeds among their crops. By late summer, the flowers were harvested, dried in the sun and shared among everyone – even with those who hadn't grown any. My mother used to roast the safflowers slowly over an open fire, then pound and rub them into a fine powder. She mixed it with roasted sesame seeds to make a special blend for *Kulêra zard* (see page 147). She lovingly called it *Darmani kulêra* (the remedy of kulêra).

JERISH (BRÊWSH)

Jerish is a popular Kurdish ingredient and a form of cracked wheat. It is different to bulgur (*saawar*) as the husk is kept whole, which means it retains more gluten and starch. This is useful as it is used for making dumplings which need gluten in them to hold everything together. You can see the difference when you boil both jerish and bulgur – bulgur will separate in the pan, but jerish will stick together.

DAIRY PRODUCTS

Dairy products feature heavily in Kurdish cuisine. One of my own favourite foods growing up was *baboula mast* (yogurt wrap). This is rehydrated *Nani tiri* (see page 146) spread with a layer of plain/natural yogurt and simply sprinkled with sugar. Mothers would wrap it up and give to their children to eat as a snack. Sheep's milk is used to make butter, yogurt, milk and *keshk* (fermented whey). Foraged herbs are added to boiled yogurt to make *zhazhi*, one of the most popular cheeses made in Kurdistan. The two ingredients are simply mixed together and then kept in a cured animal skin. This is then placed in a cool place in the mountains, such as an underground cave, to ferment while they return to their village or town. Then six months to a year later they will go back to the mountains to collect the cheese and bring it back. There are various different varieties – *zhazhi* and *paneeri kurdi* taste similar to aged Parmesan. *Zhazhi* can be mixed with butter to achieve a creamy and soft texture.

You can experience freshness on your doorstep. I made my own batch of *zhazhi* last summer by digging a hole in my London garden to keep the cheese in. It was made with wild garlic, boiled yogurt and black nigella seeds. I kept the jar in the ground for a whole year and then used the cheese when developing some of the recipes for this book – it is photographed next to the *Kulêra mezhga* (see page 148).

A tradition of foraging

There is a strong tradition of foraging in our culture. The most exciting time to forage is *Newroz* (Kurdish New Year, see page 141). At the end of winter there is a celebration called *Belen Dana* roughly translating to 'putting down the shovel' when the snow has started to melt and new life is beginning. We prepare for the coming spring by collecting the early foods, such as vine leaves to make *yapraxi bahara*, *kinger*, *kardu* and *qazwan*. We buy new material for clothes or have new clothes altered ready for their first wear in the new year.

Summer is also a time for gathering and with it comes unspoken traditions. If someone was harvesting or needing help to make food, the neighbours would spread the news by word of mouth to get as many people there to help and come together, this is called *herowes*. We would talk politics, sing, perform poetry and tell each other stories. One particular time my grandfather brought back three tractor loads of sunflower heads to our home in Qaladze. The entire neighbourhood then came down to our house with wooden sticks to be used for hitting the back of the sunflower heads to extract the seeds. It was something to do and something to be a part of. It lasted the whole evening as we gathered to play music, share stories and generally have fun together. A tray of tea would be served and it went on into the night with everyone taking some seeds home.

I carry these traditions close to me as it is what makes me who I am and strengthens my cooking. I have found wild garlic, herbs, kardu, blackberries, rose hips, vine leaves, figs, quince, green plums and many more fruits in London. Small almonds can be found in spring – pick them, dip them in salt and enjoy.

I like to share my knowledge with customers and friends about the ingredients that we find in our local green spaces. Land is land, it's important to build a connection to it, especially as our world is changing and we are becoming disconnected from it.

Basic sauces & toppings

Herb oil

2 tablespoons olive oil
1 teaspoon dried mint

Heat the oil in a frying pan/skillet, add the mint and fry for 1 minute for the herb to infuse the oil. use as a garnish to finish any dish.

* *Use any dried herb for this recipe.*

Vine leaf & qazwan sauce

10 young fresh vine leaves and shoots (stalks)
3 sliced wild shallots, pre washed and soaked, soaking water reserved
2 tablespoons pre-soaked qazwan (or capers), halved
½ thinly sliced lime
3 tablespoons olive oil
½ tablespoon salt

Put the vine leaves and shoots, shallots, qazwan or capers, lime, olive oil, salt and 3 tablespoons of the shallot water in a blender and blend well to a smooth green sauce. Pour into a saucepan and set over a medium heat. Bring to the boil, then remove from the heat and allow to cool. Transfer to a jar and keep in the fridge for up to 2 weeks.

PRE-COOKING MUTTON INSTRUCTION

Heat 1 tablespoon sunflower oil in a saucepan, add the meat and sear all over. Add ½ teaspoon salt and 750 ml/3 cups water, bring to the boil and cook for 25–30 minutes until the meat is tender. Drain, but keep the cooking liquid to use as a meat broth in other recipes.

Chilli & sumac oil

1 tablespoon butter
½ tablespoon olive oil
1 garlic clove, crushed/minced
½ teaspoon red chilli/chile, diced
½ tablespoon dried parsley
1 teaspoon sumac

To make the oil: Heat the butter and oil in a frying pan. Add the garlic and chilli and stir until soft but not browned. Add the parsley, mix, then remove from the heat. Just before serving, sprinkle the sumac on the hot oil to avoid it becoming bitter.

Salt-toasted almond flakes

¼ teaspoon salt
½ teaspoon lemon juice
1½ tablespoons flaked/slivered almonds

Mix the salt and lemon juice together in a small bowl until the salt has dissolved.

Heat a small frying pan/skillet over a medium-high heat, add the almonds and toast until lightly golden. Add the lemon juice and toss until well coated, the lemon juice has been absorbed and the almond flakes are crispy.

* *Use to garnish Kiftay brwêsh (see page 36).*

Dried kaghly topping

1 tablespoon sesame seeds
1 tablespoon nigella seeds
1 tablespoon safflower petals

Mix the seeds and safflower together in a bowl.

* *Use to sprinkle over yogurt, Xayer û mast (see page 126) and other dips.*

Menu planners

Most Kurdish dishes are designed to be part of a table spread for the whole family where everyone would share on a *xwan* (a Kurdish carpet – the word directly translates to 'tablecloth'), on the floor. We would pass the food around and enjoy the delights of variety and abundance.

There is a saying in our culture that if you have bread (*nan*), yogurt (*mast*) and grains (*dan*), you can always prepare a feast. These three staples form the base of almost every Kurdish household. Simple and fresh ingredients are key!

I have devised these menus to suggest selections of recipes to serve together, and those that will work well for different occasions and celebrations.

Newroz Picnic Menu

Newroz is the Kurdish New Year and it falls in March. We spend the entire day outdoors eating, dancing and singing. Everyone brings food to share, ready to have a fun time. It's very welcoming and sociable and strangers become friends.

BREAKFAST

Kulêra zard (Fluffy bread) p.147
Slices of melon, cucumber and tomatoes
Plain/natural yogurt
Zazhi cheese (p.129)
Chai raash (Kurdish black tea) p.159

LUNCH

Selection of grilled meats
Yapraxi silq (Mixed stuffed vegetables) p.27
Kubay brinj (Kurdish rice dumplings) p.32
Shiftay gosht (Spiced beef patties) p.43
Zalatay shwani (Shepherd's salad) p.142
Tirshyat kurdi (Crunchy pickled vegetables) p.120
Nani tiri (Flat wafer bread) p.146

DINNER (USING LEFTOVERS)

Goshtaw (Lamb & chilli stew) p.71
Fresh green herbs, lemon wedges and roasted sunflower seeds
Chai raash (Kurdish black tea) p.159

Festive Celebration Menu

This selection of dishes would be used to create a special meal for any kind of celebration, whether that's for a birthday, anniversary, special get-together or even to celebrate New Year's Eve.

Parda pilaw (Rice & meat pie) p.103
Gipay mreeshk (Chicken stuffed with spicy rice & nuts) p.84
Gipay parasû (Spiced aromatic rice with lamb) p.114
Xayar û mast (Yogurt & cucumber dip) p.126
Fresh Romaine lettuce dressed with organic red wine vinegar
Salted walnuts (see below)
Roasted sunflower seeds
Xoshaw (Dried fruit drink & dessert) p.158
Kwlicha gwêz (Sweet stuffed dough parcels) p.164

To make salted walnuts: place 150 g/5½ oz. walnuts in a jar with 2 tablespoons salt and fill the jar with water. Leave for 1–2 days, then drain, return to the jar with more water and a further 2 tablespoons salt. Do this once more after 1–2 days, then drain, return to the jar, add 1 tablespoon salt and only half-fill the jar with water. Store in the fridge for up to 1–2 weeks and enjoy with salads, Xayer û mast (see page 126) or as a snack with drinks.

Jezhin (Eid) Celebration Menu

This menu reminds me of Jezhin celebrations growing up, when we would wake early in the morning to the smell of sweet apricots and cinnamon cooking in the house.

Shley qeysi (Slow-cooked apricot stew) p.60
Qibuli kurdi (Rice with chickpeas & caramelized onions) p.106
Selection of fresh salad and herbs
Parda pilaw (Rice & meat pie) p.103
Tamata û bamya (Okra, meat & tomato stew) p.59
Zalatay shwani (Shepherd's salad) p.142
Dowkuliw be punga (Yogurt soup) p.52
Tirshyat kurdi (Crunchy pickled vegetables) p.120
Kwlicha gwêz (Sweet stuffed dough parcels) p.164

Busy Weeknight Menu

This is the perfect menu for those busy nights when you still want some quick and satisfying food.

Shiftay gosht (Spiced beef patties) p.43
Brinji sûr (Red rice) p.112
Zalatay shwani (Shepherd's salad) p.142
Fresh herbs and salad (watercress, baby leeks, mint)
Mastaw (Yogurt, mint & dill drink) p.160

Restorative Menu

Cook these dishes for anyone recuperating from an illness or for someone who has recently given birth and needs some sustenance.

Niskêna (Red lentil soup) p.48
Mashêna (Mung bean & barley soup topped with a poached egg) p.51
Helkaw (Egg & lentil soup) p.55
Frujaw (Chicken & potato stew) p.79
Kulêra zard (Fluffy bread) p.147
Zalatay tirsha piyaz (Onion salad) p.142

Weekend Brunch Menu

A wonderful spread for a lazy weekend brunch with friends and family.

Basirmay bainjan (Pan-fried tomato & aubergine) p.91
Kulêra saawar (Fried bulgur patties) p.40
Niskêna (Red lentil soup) p.48
Silqi surkrawa (Pan-fried Swiss chard with poached eggs) p.95
Brinji sûr (Red rice) p.112
Masi surkrawa (Fried fish with sumac) p.99
Kinger masi (Fried kinger patties) p.137
Zalatay kuzala (Watercress, radish & pomegranate salad) p.141
Shêlm be tirsh (Fermented beetroot, turnip & carrots) p. 125
Shilkêna (Kurdish pancakes) p.167

Wedding Party Menu

This selection of dishes can be used to create a 4- or 5-course meal perfect for any wedding celebration.

Yapraxi silq (Mixed stuffed vegetables) p.27
and Yapraxi bahara (Stuffed vine leaves) p.35
Kifta û shorbaw (Rice & beef dumplings cooked in meaty broth) p.24
Pilaw (Basmati rice with bread layer) p.107
Gipay mreeshk (Chicken stuffed with spicy rice & nuts) p.84
Gipay parasû (Spiced aromatic rice with lamb) p.114
Niskêna (Red lentil soup) p.48
Xayar û mast (Yogurt & cucumber dip) p.126
Tirshyat kurdi (Crunchy pickled vegetables) p.120
Zalatay shwani (Shepherd's salad) p.142
Kwlicha gwêz (Sweet stuffed dough parcels) p.164
Chai raash (Kurdish black tea) p.159
Xoshaw (Dried fruit drink & dessert) p.158

Dolma & dumplings

Tichma bainjan û xayar

تیچمە باینجان و خەیار

STUFFED AUBERGINE & CUCUMBERS

This recipe features aubergines/eggplants and cucumber stuffed with diced meat, rice and spices. In Kurdistan, when I was a young child, I rarely travelled outside my hometown of Qaladze in the east. The only other place I ever visited was Ranya, about half an hour away; that was the longest distance I ever travelled. I had been to Slemani in eastern Kurdistan, but never to the capital, Hewlêr. This dish belongs to Hewlêr. The first time I ate this was when I got married, and we had come back from Rojhelat in eastern Kurdistan. We visited my brother-in-law for the first time. When we got there, we bumped into an old friend of my husband's who insisted that we come to dinner with him and his family. So we went to his home, and his wife cooked *tichma*. It was stuffed like a dolma, but it was a cucumber. She didn't eat cucumber, so she made hers with aubergine. It was delicious, especially the filling inside. There weren't many spices, so the aubergine dyed the rice purple. It was very meaty – it was heaven. It was my first time trying this dish.

2 long aubergines/eggplants
2 cucumbers
salt and freshly ground black pepper

FILLING

1 tablespoon olive oil (or sunflower oil)
700 g/1½ lb. lamb meat (shoulder or leg), diced into small pieces (or any red meat will be fine)
1 teaspoon salt
½ tablespoon freshly ground black pepper
¼ teaspoon ground allspice
240 g/1⅓ cups short-grain rice washed

SAUCE

1 tablespoon sunflower oil
500 g/1 lb. 2 oz. lamb meat (shoulder or leg), cut into chunks
2 tablespoons tomato purée/paste
2 tomatoes, largely diced
1 onion, largely diced
½ teaspoon freshly ground black pepper
1 small hot green chilli/chile, diced
½ tablespoon salt (or to taste)

TO GARNISH

dollop of yogurt (optional)
finely chopped chives or parsley
2 tablespoons pine nuts, roasted

white thread and needle (or use toothpicks/cocktail sticks)

SERVES 4

Roughly 10 minutes before you start to cook, wash and prepare the aubergine and cucumber. Cut them in half, widthways, and use a spoon to remove the flesh to create a hollow vessel. Cut the flesh into small chunks, season with salt and pepper and set aside in a bowl until needed.

Prepare the filling. Heat the oil in a frying pan/skillet over a medium heat. Add the diced meat and stir-fry to a golden brown. Add the salt, pepper and allspice, mix well and cook until tender. Remove the meat from the heat, mix with the drained rice and set aside.

Make the sauce. Heat the oil in a large saucepan over a high heat, add the meat and fry for 3–4 minutes. Add the tomato purée and stir to avoid burning. Pour in 1 litre/4 cups water, stir until combined, then add the tomatoes, onion, black pepper, green chilli and salt. Turn the heat down to medium-high, add the reserved flesh of the vegetables and taste if it needs more salt and pepper. Cover and let simmer while you finish preparing the aubergines and cucumbers.

Stuff the vegetable shells with the filling, leaving about 2 cm/1 inch from the top clear to allow the rice to expand without overfilling. Sew the vegetables shut by hand to avoid any filling coming out.

One by one, gently drop the vegetables into the sauce, mix them around and cook for 20–25 minutes until they are tender and soft. Make sure the sauce has thickened and is not too thin or very thick.

To serve, put the sauce and vegetables in a bowl, then remove the thread from the aubergines and cucumber, cut them into large pieces and place on top of the sauce. Sprinkle over some chopped chives or parsley and roasted pine nuts. This can also be served individually with a dollop of yogurt on the side and garnished with fresh herbs and roasted pine nuts.

Bainjan in the winter months

In Kurdistan, drying vegetables is a popular tradition. We do this so we can enjoy vegetables all year round. Some of these vegetables are aubergines/eggplants, okra and courgette/zucchini (and sun-dried tomatoes). Dried aubergine and courgette is especially useful in winter to create favourite dishes, such as yapraxi bainjan *(aubergine dolma). My great aunt was well known for her* yapraxi bainjan. *The rice would turn purple, there was sourness from the sumac and the aroma was earthy and delicious. It didn't matter what dish she made, when she used aubergine, you could tell it was her food.*

Kifta û shorbaw

كفته و شۆرباو

RICE & BEEF DUMPLINGS COOKED IN MEATY BROTH

The key to the success of this dish is kneading the dough for long enough so that it sticks together – this shouldn't be rushed!

DUMPLING SHELL

250 g/9 oz. minced/ground beef (7% fat)
120 g/2⅔ cups short-grain rice, soaked for 30 minutes, drained
1 teaspoon salt
1 teaspoon ground black pepper
1 teaspoon ground cumin

FILLING

150 g/5½ oz. minced/ground beef
1 large onion, peeled and finely diced
1 teaspoon ground cumin
1 teaspoon ground turmeric
1 teaspoon ground allspice
1 teaspoon freshly ground black pepper
½ teaspoon dried chilli flakes/ hot red pepper flakes
½ teaspoon ground cloves
½ tablespoon salt
50 g/1⅔ cup chopped fresh parsley
40 g/⅓ cup sultanas/golden raisins
40 g/⅓ cup blanched almonds

SAUCE (STEW)

2 tablespoons olive oil
1 onion, peeled and diced
250 g/9 oz. lamb on the bone (shoulder, neck or leg)
½ teaspoon ground turmeric
2 small mild green chillies/chiles
140 g/1 cup part-cooked chickpeas (see page 67 for cooking method)
2 dried limes (or ½ lemon, sliced)
½ teaspoon salt
½ teaspoon ground black pepper
Dried kaghly topping (see page 15), to serve

SERVES 4–5

Mix the beef mince, rice, salt, pepper and cumin together in a bowl. Knead together for 15–20 minutes until the mixture resembles a smooth dough. Alternatively, to save time, blend everything in a food processor or blender for 10–15 minutes to a smooth consistency. Set aside to rest.

For the filling, sear the beef in a frying pan/skillet over a medium-high heat until the meat has browned, then add 65 ml/¼ cup water and stir so the water can help the mince to separate. Cook, stirring occasionally, until the meat is cooked and you can smell the aroma of the mince.

Add the onion, stir, then add all the spices and salt and mix together. Taste and adjust the seasoning if needed. Remove from the heat and stir in the parsley, sultanas and almonds, mix, then set aside to cool.

For the sauce, heat the olive oil in a large saucepan over a medium heat, add the onion and cook until softened and golden. Add the meat and the spices, mix together and sear the meat until golden brown. Add 2 litres/ 8 cups water and bring to the boil. Add the chickpeas, dried lime, salt and pepper, then turn down the heat and simmer, covered, over a low heat.

Meanwhile, start on the dumplings. Divide the shell mixture into 5 equal portions, the size of a small apple. Wet your hands with a little water and place a portion of the mixture in the palm of your hand. Roll into a ball, then use the thumb of your other hand to make an indentation in the centre of the ball and continue pressing the mixture to shape it into an evenly shaped cup. Put 2 tablespoons of the filling in the centre of the dumpling and bring the edges of the dough together to enclose the filling. Shape each dumpling into a ball and place on a baking sheet.

Once all the dumplings are formed, gently lower them into the simmering sauce. With a flat spatula move the dumplings so they don't stick to the bottom, cook for 30 minutes, then check the seasoning, adding more salt and pepper if needed.

Once the dumplings start floating, the meat is tender and the chickpeas are soft it is ready to serve. Place in a serving bowl and sprinkle over the dried kaghly topping to finish.

NOTE *This is also delicious drizzled with Sir û mast (see page 126).*

Yapraxi silq

یاپراخی سڵق

MIXED STUFFED VEGETABLES

This is a staple Kurdish dish recognized in all regions. It's also prepared at home and taken on *sayran* (see page 96) outings (picnics) and cooked outdoors over a wood-fired flame. This dish is also popular during spring, once the first vegetables and herbs of the season have been harvested. There are even competitions between family members to see who can make the best *yaprax* with their harvest!

2 onions
1 aubergine/eggplant, long and thin preferably (keep the head of the aubergine, pierce a few holes with the tip of a knife to allow water to escape)
1 courgette/zucchini,
2 small green (bell) peppers
2 tomatoes
3 tablespoons rapeseed oil
3 garlic cloves, finely chopped
1 chilli/chile, diced (any colour)
2½ tablespoons tomato purée/paste
juice of 1 lemon
2 tablespoons ground sumac
1 teaspoon ground turmeric
1 teaspoon ground cumin
1 teaspoon freshly ground black pepper
1 teaspoon dried chilli flakes/hot red pepper flakes
2 teaspoons salt
400 g/2¼ cups short-grain rice, washed until water runs clear
bunch of fresh dill (about 100 g/3½ oz.)
100 g/3½ oz. celery leaves (can substitute with parsley)
3–4 tablespoons chopped fresh thyme (about 10 g/⅓ oz.)
3–4 tablespoons chopped fresh oregano (about 10 g/⅓ oz.)

Start with preparing the vegetables. For the onion, remove the top and bottom, cutting into the onion at a slight angle to take out some of the core, then cut down one side to the centre. This will make it easier to peel off the layers once it's boiled. Remove the skin and boil it in a saucepan of water for 15–20 minutes, ensuring it is completely submerged, until soft.

Cut the top of the aubergine off and hollow it out using a knife and then a teaspoon. Remove most of the flesh but leave enough to ensure the aubergine can hold the filling without tearing.

Peel the courgette in stripes, trim off the top and de-core it, then dice the peel and flesh very finely and set aside to use later in the filling.

Cut around the top of the green peppers to make a lid, remove the seeds and do the same for the tomatoes.

Pierce all of the vegetables a few times with a sharp knife to help the steaming process once filled.

Heat 1 tablespoon of the oil in a large saucepan over a medium heat. Add the hollowed out aubergine, courgette and peppers and cook for about 5 minutes to sear and soften them. Remove from the pan and set aside.

Add 2 tablespoons of the oil to the same large saucepan over a medium heat, add the diced courgette, garlic and chilli and sauté for 5 minutes until golden brown. Add the tomato purée, lemon juice, spices and salt, mix well and fry for 3–5 minutes.

Add the fried mixture to the drained rice along with the fresh herbs, sultanas and a little salt. Mix it together until combined.

Peel apart the boiled onions, take each layer apart carefully, and place them aside individually. Take one onion layer, place 1 tablespoon of the filling in the middle of the layer and roll it up to enclose the filling, making sure it's tightly rolled. Repeat with all the onion layers.

Recipe continued overleaf ››

30 g/¼ cup sultanas/golden raisins, chopped
500 g/1 lb. 2 oz. Swiss chard, washed, stalks removed and leaves cut in half
150 g/5½ oz. fresh green broad/fava beans or green beans
70 g/⅓ cup/⅔ stick butter, cubed
chopped fresh parsley, to garnish

SERVES 6

Fill the other hollowed out vegetables (aubergine, courgette, green peppers and tomatoes) with about 2 tablespoons of the rice mixture, leaving a 1-cm/½-inch gap near the top to allow for the rice to expand during the cooking process.

Once the vegetables have been stuffed, replace the top of the vegetables to make the vegetable whole again, and avoid the rice spilling out during the cooking process.

To make the Swiss chard rolls, place the Swiss chard leaves flat on the work top, add ½ tablespoon of the rice mixture horizontally along one edge and roll it.

Using the same pan that was used for the rice filling mixture, place the Swiss chard stalks and the broad beans on the base, then add the stuffed onions layers, stuffed aubergine, courgette, peppers and tomatoes firmly beside each other. The stuffed Swiss chard will be the final vegetable roll to be placed in the pan at the top, as it is the softest and needs the shortest cooking time.

Place a plate with a slightly smaller diameter than the pan on top of the vegetables, to act as a weight to hold all the vegetables together.

Add 1 litre/4 cups water (it shouldn't rise above the plate sitting at the top). Let it simmer for 20 minutes and once the water starts bubbling, turn down the heat, cover and cook for a further 10 minutes.

Remove the plate, add the cubes of butter around the top and cook for a further 5–10 minutes. Check the top layer to ensure the rice is soft and cooked. Once it's ready, remove from the heat and rest for 10 minutes before serving.

To serve, place a large serving platter over the pan, ensuring the pan is completely covered. Carefully invert the pan and serving platter and slowly lift the pan to reveal the stuffed vegetables with the broad beans at the top. Garnish with chopped parsley.

Serve with soft flatbreads, Mastaw (see page 160), Xayer û mast (see page 126), fresh herbs and pickles.

Doghawa

دۆغاوه

MEAT DUMPLINGS COOKED IN YOGURT BROTH

This recipe is shared by both the north and the south of Kurdistan today and is also known as *kutlke dew*. This particular version is a southern fusion, specifically from Hewlêr, which is the capital of Kurdistan.

DUMPLING SHELL

150 g/¾ cup short-grain rice, soak for 30 minutes, then drain
350 g/12 oz. jerish cracked wheat or bulgur wheat, washed, covered and left to soak for 45 minutes or until soft
½ tablespoon salt
½ teaspoon ground cumin
1 egg

SAUCE

1 heaped teaspoon plain/all-purpose flour
1 egg, beaten
500 g/2⅓ cups Greek yogurt
1 litre/4 cups beef broth or any red meat broth

FILLING

2 tablespoons olive oil
500 g/1 lb. 2 oz. minced/ground mutton (7% fat)
1 large onion, peeled and finely diced
70 g/½ cup raisins
70 g/½ cup almonds, blanched and skinned
1 teaspoon ground cumin
1 teaspoon ground allspice
1 teaspoon ground cloves
50 g/1½ cups chopped flat celery leaves (or use parsley)
salt and freshly ground black pepper

TO GARNISH

chopped spring onions/scallions
2 teaspoons dried oregano
pinch of safflower petals

SERVES 4–5

First, prepare the dough for the dumplings. Put the drained rice in a blender and pulse to break down the rice. Add the jerish, salt, cumin and egg and blend until it's all mixed together. It should form a nice smooth dough. Transfer to a mixing bowl and knead for 5–7 minutes. Divide the dough into 6–8 even-sized balls, cover to prevent drying out and set aside to rest while you prepare the sauce.

Mix the flour with 500 ml/2 cups water, then slowly pour in the egg and yogurt and mix until combined.

Heat a saucepan over a medium heat, add the yogurt mixture and slowly add the broth, stirring continuously, until the mixture starts to boil. When the sauce starts to bubble remove from the heat and set aside.

Now, prepare the filling. Heat the oil in a frying pan/skillet over a medium-high heat. Add the mutton and use a wooden spoon to break the meat up as it cooks, stirring until all the liquid has evaporated. Add the onion, stir well, then add all the remaining ingredients, except the celery leaves. Fry for about 5 minutes, then season with salt and pepper to taste. Remove from the heat, stir in the celery leaves and drain to remove any excess liquid.

To form the dumplings, take one of the dough balls in the palm of your hand. Roll into a ball, then use the thumb of your other hand to make an indentation in the centre of the ball and continue pressing the mixture to shape it into an evenly shaped cup.

Place 1½ tablespoons of the filling in the dough cup. Gather the dough at the top and pinch together to form a little purse. Gently flatten the dumpling to a 2-cm/¾-inch thick round. Repeat with the remaining dough. You should have some leftover filling, set aside.

Reheat the sauce and bring to a gentle boil. Add the dumplings to the sauce, stir gently to avoid them sticking to the bottom and cook for 45–60 minutes. Once they start floating, add salt and pepper to taste, spring onions, dried oregano and any leftover filling and cook for a further 15 minutes, before serving. Garnish with a pinch of safflower petals.

Kubay brinj

كوبەی برینج

KURDISH RICE DUMPLINGS

These Kurdish crispy rice dumplings can be stuffed with any meat or vegetable. They are perfect served as an appetizer or as part of a mezze table.

DUMPLING SHELL

- 1½ tablespoons salt
- 300 g/1½ cups short-grain rice
- 1 small egg (optional)
- 500 ml/2 cups sunflower oil, for frying

FILLING

- 2 tablespoons olive oil or sunflower oil
- 200 g/7 oz. minced/ground beef
- 1 large onion, peeled and finely diced
- 20 g/¾ oz. raisins
- 20 g/¾ oz. whole almonds, blanched and halved
- ½ tablespoon freshly ground black pepper
- ½ teaspoon ground turmeric
- ½ teaspoon ground allspice
- ½ teaspoon ground cumin
- ½ tablespoon salt
- bunch of parsley, finely chopped

TO SERVE

- lettuce
- Vine leaf & qazwan sauce (see page 15)

MAKES 10–12

Fill a saucepan with 1.5 litres/6 cups water and bring to the boil. Add the salt, mix, then add the rice, stir and bring back to the boil. Simmer for 5–7 minutes until the rice is tender but not over cooked. Remove from the heat, drain and put somewhere cold to cool while you start with the filling.

Heat the oil in a frying pan/skillet over a medium heat, add the beef and fry until all the water has been absorbed and the meat is slightly brown, breaking it up as it cooks. Add the onion and stir through the meat, then stir in the raisins and almonds and mix together. Add all the spices and salt, mix together, then remove from the heat and stir in the parsley.

Place the cooked rice in a bowl, add the egg, if using, and knead the rice into a nice smooth dough, then divide into 10–12 egg-size balls.

Wet your hands with a drop of water and oil. Take one rice ball and flatten between your palms, forming an indentation in the centre of the ball and shaping the dough into and oval shape.

Place 2 tablespoons of the beef filling in the centre of each ball. Bring the sides together and close the rice dough around the filling. Gently shape the dumpling into an egg shape, then place on a baking sheet.

Heat the oil for frying in a heavy-based deep frying pan over a medium-high heat and heat to 170°C/320°F . Carefully add the dumplings, 4 at a time, and fry for 3–5 minutes until nice and crispy on the outside and soft inside. Place on paper towel to drain the excess oil.

To serve, place the lettuce on a platter with a bowl of the qazwan sauce in the middle and arrange the dumplings around the sauce ready for dipping.

NOTES

- *If you don't want to use egg in the rice shell, put the dumplings in the freezer for 10 minutes to set before frying.*
- *To make* kuba parû *(a wrap with bread or lettuce), wrap the dumplings in the lettuce, drizzle with sauce and top with slices of gherkins.*
- *You can also add a small bowl of rich black grape vinegar to serve.*

Yapraxi bahara

یاپراخی بەهارە

STUFFED VINE LEAVES

In Kurdistan, *yapraxi bahara* (which translates to 'spring dolma') is a sign of spring. We make it with the first vine leaves from the spring season. Inside, it's packed with fresh spring onions/scallions, broad/fava beans, herbs and creamy sheeps' yogurt mixed with rice and dill. There's a tradition where villages compete to make the smallest rolls, called *danke nulq* (a 'wrapped-up little sweet'). Generally everyone would show off their *yapraxi bahara* at picnics, especially at Newroz, and would compete to see whose was the best.

4 tablespoons olive or sunflower oil
500 g/1 lb. 2 oz. lamb ribs, seasoned with salt and pepper
1 tablespoon salt
1 teaspoon ground black pepper
1 large onion, peel and finely diced
300 g/1½ cups short-grain rice, rinsed and drained
350 g/1½ cups plain/natural yogurt
bunch of fresh dill, washed and finely chopped
20 g/¾ oz. chopped flat celery leaves (or parsley)
10 g/¼ oz. chopped fresh oregano leaves (or dried oregano)
10 g/¼ oz. chopped fresh thyme
bunch of spring onions/scallions, finely chopped
½ teaspoon ground turmeric
juice of 1 lemon
3 garlic cloves, finely diced
200 g/1¾ cups broad/fava beans, washed
1 kg/2¼ lb. fresh vine leaves, washed and dried 1 hour before use to soften
2 tablespoons butter

a heavy ceramic heatproof flat plate

SERVES 4–5

Heat 1 tablespoon of the oil in a large saucepan over a medium heat and sear the pre-seasoned lamb ribs with a pinch of salt and ½ teaspoon black pepper for a couple of minutes on each side. Set aside.

To make the filling, heat the remaining oil in the same saucepan, and fry the onion until golden brown. Transfer to a mixing bowl and add the rice, yogurt, herbs, spring onion, turmeric, a little salt, lemon juice and garlic and stir well until all combined.

Line the base of the same deep pan with the broad beans and sprinkle with a little salt, then top with the seared lamb ribs.

Place a vine leaf on the flat plate, vine side up. Place a heaped teaspoon of the filling in the middle of the leaf near the stem, then fold both sides of the leaf towards the middle. Fold the stem end up over the filling and fold the bottom of the leaf onto the stem and roll it into a small square parcel. Repeat until you have used up all the mixture.

Place the stuffed vine leaves on top of the ribs, making sure there is no space between them, then place a ceramic heatproof plate on top. Pour in 1 litre/4 cups water, making sure the water reaches the bottom of the plate, then cover with a lid. Set the pan over a medium heat and cook for 10–15 minutes until bubbling, then turn the heat down and cook for a further 10 minutes. Remove the plate, dot the butter over the top and check if more water is needed by opening up one of the dolmas to see if the rice is cooked. Cook for a few more minutes with the lid on, then turn off the heat and let sit for about 5 minutes before serving.

Serving in the traditional way requires a bit of technique. Place a large plate on top of the pan and flip the pan over so the contents are tipped onto the plate with the lamb ribs on top.

You can serve it with fresh salad, Sir û mast (see page 126) and softened Nani tiri (see page 146), sprinkling water over the wafer breads to make the bread softer.

Kiftay brwêsh

كفته برويّش

LAMB DUMPLINGS COOKED IN SWISS CHARD BROTH

In some areas, like Hewlêr, they cook this with beetroot so the sauce turns red, and they call it *silqa sûr*. In Duhok province, they make it with turnip, pumpkin, potatoes and meat and call it *avshirin* (sweet water) and the broth is white.

DUMPLING SHELLS

200 g/1¼ cups jerish cracked wheat, soaked for 20 minutes to soften, then drained
100 ml/scant ½ cup warm water
100 g/⅔ cup short-grain rice, soaked for 20 minutes
1 teaspoon salt
½ teaspoon each ground turmeric, cumin and black pepper

FILLING

200 g/7 oz. minced/ground lamb
1 large onion, peeled and finely diced
1 teaspoon each of salt, ground black pepper, allspice, coriander and turmeric
40 g/⅓ cup raisins
35 g/¼ cup blanched almonds
35 g/1 cup chopped parsley

BROTH

2 tablespoons olive oil
1 large onion, peeled and thinly sliced
2 garlic cloves, finely diced
2½ tablespoons tomato purée
2.5 litres/quarts hot water
50 g/1¼ cups part-cooked yellow split chickpeas (see page 55)
1 teaspoon black pepper
1 teaspoon salt
juice of ½ sour pomegranate
230 g/8 oz. Swiss chard, washed and finely chopped
2 large tomatoes, chopped into small chunks
Salt-toasted Almonds (see page 15)

SERVES 4

To make the dumpling shells, put the jerish in a bowl and wash with warm water, then drain. Add the warm water and soak for 15 minutes to soften.

For the filling, put the lamb in a frying pan/skillet, over a medium-high heat, then use a wooden spoon to break up any chunks. Once the mince starts to brown, add the onion and mix together. Add the salt, pepper and ground spices and stir until combined. Add the raisins and almonds and fry for 2–3 minutes. Remove from the heat, then mix in the chopped parsley. Leave to cool for 10 minutes.

For the shells, drain the rice and break it up in a bowl with your hands. Add the jerish, salt and spices, mix together, then transfer to a blender and blend until the mixture forms a smooth dough. Divide the dough into 6–7 balls. Take one ball at the time and flatten it in the palm of your hand.

Place a spoonful of the filling in the middle of the dough, then bring the edges up and over to completely enclose the filling and form a ball. Press and flatten the dumpling between your hands to make a disc. Repeat this for the other dough balls and place them all on a baking sheet. Cover to prevent drying out while you prepare the broth.

Heat the oil in a large pan over a medium heat. Add the onion and garlic and sauté for 2–3 minutes. Add the tomato purée and stir-fry for a further minute. Add the hot water, split chickpeas, black pepper, salt, pomegranate juice, Swiss chard and tomatoes and bring to the boil.

Slowly add the dumplings to the sauce and cook for 5 minutes, then stir slowly to avoid them sticking to the bottom. Turn the heat down and cook until the dumplings start floating to the top, the Swiss chard, split chickpeas are cooked and the sauce has been reduced.

Serve the dumplings in a bowl, garnished with salt-toasted almonds.

NOTES

- *You can use lemon juice instead of pomegranate juice and serve with lemon wedges for squeezing over at the end if liked.*
- *If the jerish dough is too dry, add 2 tablespoons water to soften.*
- *If it's hard to make the dumpling shell, wear rubber gloves and rub a bit of oil on your hands to help shape the dumplings.*

Givishk

گفیشک

BEEF & RICE SAUSAGES

As a Kurdish nation we have many dialects, different religions and different ethnic minorities. We have many different styles and colours of clothes and different ways of life. We are a diverse culture, but we have a strong identity. *Givishk* is a good example of this with every region of Kurdistan having its own take on this dish. This particular version is from the Badinan region.

First, make the sausages. Place the rice, beef, salt, black pepper, allspice, half the black basil and the grated onion in a large bowl and mix together. Knead for about 5 minutes until combined into a smooth dough.

Take a meatball-sized amount of the mixture in the palm of your hand and shape and squeeze the dough into a little sausage shape, but with the shape of your fingers imprinted on them. Repeat until you use up all the mixture, placing the sausages on a baking sheet.

In a medium shallow cooking pan, layer the vegetables (potato, onion, tomato, white part of the spring onions, broad beans, green pepper) on the base of the pan, sprinkle over the remaining black basil and top with the sausages.

Strain the sumac water (discarding the pulp) and pour it over the sausage. Place the pan over a medium heat.

Mix the bone broth, turmeric, cumin, 1 tablespoon of the olive oil and some salt and pepper in a small bowl and pour it into the pan. Set over a medium heat, cover with a lid and simmer for 15 minutes.

When the rice is cooked it will look fluffy on the outside of the sausages. Remove one and taste to check the rice is completely cooked, heating for a little longer if necessary.

Pour the herb oil over the sausages, cover and cook for 5–10 minutes.

To serve, arrange the vegetables on a serving plate with the sausage on top and pour over the sauce from the vegetables. Drizzle Sir û mast over the sausages very lightly and drizzle with the Chilli sumac oil. Garnish with finely chopped spring onions to finish.

NOTE *Instead of short-grain rice, you could use risotto rice, pudding rice or jasmine rice.*

1 potato, peeled and cut into cubes
1 large onion, peeled and thinly sliced
1 large tomato, peeled and cut into chunks
1 bunch of spring onions/scallions, divided into two parts (white part cut into 2 pieces and green bits finely chopped)
130 g/4½ oz. fine young broad/fava beans, washed and cut in half
1 long sweet green pepper, deseeded cut to chunks
1½ tablespoons sumac dissolved into 240 ml/1 cup water
480 ml/2 cups bone broth
1 teaspoon ground turmeric
1 teaspoon ground cumin
2½ tablespoons olive oil
1½ tablespoons Herb oil (see page 15), made with dried parsley
salt and freshly ground black pepper

SAUSAGES

150 g/¾ cup short-grain rice, soaked, drained and dried
350 g/12½ oz. minced/ground beef
1 tablespoon salt
1 tablespoon freshly ground black pepper
½ teaspoon ground allspice
½ tablespoon black basil
1 onion, peeled and grated

TO SERVE

Sir û mast (see page 126)
Chilli sumac oil (see page 15)

SERVES 4

Kulêra saawar

كولێره ساوار

FRIED BULGUR PATTIES

These delicate patties are ideal served for breakfast with a fried egg. They are often mistaken for having been made with quinoa due to the texture. Also known as *pirxaneela*, the name translates to a mix of *pir* (elderly) and *xaneela* (happy or happy elders), which is very apt as the soft texture makes it ideal for the elderly and also young children.

250 g/1½ cups fine bulgur, washed and drained
2 tomatoes, chopped
1 onion, peeled and finely diced
bunch of chopped fresh parsley (about 50 g/1¾ oz.)
100 g/3½ oz. chopped spring onions/scallions
bunch of chopped fresh dill (about 50 g/1¾ oz.)
1 teaspoon salt
½ teaspoon ground turmeric
½ teaspoon freshly ground black pepper
70 g/½ cup plain/all-purpose flour
1 tablespoon olive oil
vegetable oil, for brushing

MAKES ABOUT 8–10

Place the bulgur in a large bowl. Add the chopped tomatoes and diced onion and knead it together.

Add the remaining ingredients, except the vegetable oil, to the kneaded dough and combine to form a smooth soft dough. Cover with a clean cloth and set aside to rest for 2–3 minutes.

Meanwhile, preheat a cast-iron pan/skillet. Brush the pan with oil.

Make about 8–10 small round balls from the dough. Take a ball and carefully flatten it onto the base of the hot pan. Flatten it into a small disc about 10–15 cm/4–6 inches wide (remember to cover your fingertips or palm with oil to prevent stickiness). Cook for 3–5 minutes on each side.

Enjoy with a sweet black tea, or serve with a fried egg or yogurt.

NOTE *If you can't find bulgur, you can use coarse semolina instead.*

Xarman –the wheat harvest

Wheat is harvested in late summer. It's usually divided into 10 kg/22 lb. cans (teneka) *and then divided into smaller portions. Some of the wheat will go to the mill to make flour and some will be kept to make* cracked wheat/bulgur *for use throughout the year. Early in the morning, the wheat is boiled in big pots over an open fire, until it becomes soft and is then placed in a big sieve/strainer called a* sabata *that is made out of fine willow wood. It is then taken to the roof terrace, where a big blanket, called a* chader*, is laid out and the cooked wheat is spread out on top to dry in the sun. In the evening, the chader is folded over to cover the wheat to stop any animals eating it in the night. Early the next morning, the wheat is uncovered again to continue drying. This continues for 3 days until the wheat has fully dried. The dried wheat is then ground by hand into a coarse* saawar *(bulgur) to last through to the next harvest, or a very fine* saawar*, which is used to make* pirxaneela.

Shiftay gosht

شفتەی گۆشت

SPICED BEEF PATTIES

These lightly spiced patties would be served for lunch and dinner. Typically many would be made at the same time and then stuffed into bread to make *nan parû* (bites) with many fresh herbs (particularly watercress), raw onions, pickles and pan-fried tomatoes to make a filling meal. It is also delicious paired with Niskêna (see page 48).

- 750 g/1 lb. 10 oz. minced/ground beef (10% fat)
- bunch of fresh parsley, finely chopped (about 100 g/3½ oz.)
- 1 large onion, peeled and finely diced
- 2 tomatoes, deseeded and grated (no water)
- 2 teaspoons salt
- 4 garlic cloves, crushed/minced
- 1½ teaspoons freshly ground black pepper
- 1 tablespoon ground sumac
- 2 tablespoons plain/all-purpose flour
- 1 tablespoon tomato purée/paste
- 500 ml/2 cups vegetable or sunflower oil

MAKES ABOUT 15

Mix all the ingredients, except the oil, together in a large bowl. Knead into a dough once all combined.

Have a bowl of cold water next to you. Take an egg-sized ball of meat and flatten it between your palms to make a long patty roughly the length of your hand, about 6 cm/2½ inches wide, making sure the sides are neat.

Place the patties on a baking sheet while you finish using all the mixture.

Heat the vegetable or sunflower oil in a frying pan/skillet over a medium-high heat. To test if the oil is ready to use, drop a tiny bit of the meat mixture into the oil; if it floats to the top, it is ready for frying.

Fry the patties for 1½ minutes on each side, then remove with a slotted spoon or tongs and place on a plate lined with paper towels to absorb any excess oil.

Serve alongside red rice or Niskêna (see page 48), Zalatay shwani (see page 142), with pickles and Mastaw (see page 160).

ATLAS

Soups & stews

Trxêna

ترخێنه

LENTIL & BEAN SOUP

This is a hearty soup made with Tarasaz (see page 122, and pictured opposite). Usually this dish is cooked in autumn/fall and winter because of the amount of energy it can provide. As our land was very cold and snowy during these seasons, *trxêna* would be cooked overnight in a clay pot. The night before, all the ingredients are placed in the pot and the lid would be covered with butter and water and a dough to seal it. The pot would then be put in a *tandur*, with the lid covered with mud or soil and then left to slowly cook for 8 hours. It is still made this way in some parts of Kurdistan. *Pictured on pages 44–45.*

- 1 tablespoon rapeseed oil
- 300 g/10½ oz. sheep meat chunks, part-cooked (see page 15 for cooking instructions)
- 1 onion, peeled and diced
- 1½ tablespoons tomato purée/paste
- 1 portion (about 200 g/7 oz.) of Tarasaz (see page 122)
- 15 g/½ oz. fresh or dried skin from a Galia melon, finely chopped (optional)
- 25 g/1 oz. part-cooked chickpeas (see page 55 for cooking instructions)
- 25 g/1 oz. green lentils
- 20 g/¾ oz. black eye beans
- 20 g/¾ oz. walnuts
- 20 g/¾ oz. whole almonds, soaked and skins removed
- 15 g/½ oz. dried apricots, halved
- 15 g/½ oz. dried apples or pears
- 20 g/¾ oz. jumbo black raisins
- 10 g/¼ oz. dried cranberries
- 15 g/½ oz. dried sour cherries
- 1 beetroot, skinned and diced
- 1 tablespoon salt (or to taste)

TOPPING

- 1 slice of pumpkin, cubed
- ½ tablespoon olive oil
- ½ teaspoon sea salt
- ½ teaspoon freshly ground black pepper

CRISPY ONIONS

- 1 tablespoon butter
- 1 tablespoon rapeseed oil
- 1 onion, peeled and finely sliced

TO GARNISH

- 1 tablespoon toasted flaked/slivered almonds, to garnish
- 2 tablespoons fresh cranberries

SERVES 4

Preheat the oven to 180°C/350°F/gas 4.

First, make the topping. Mix the pumpkin with the oil, salt and pepper in a bowl and then spread out on a baking sheet. Bake in the preheated oven for 25 minutes, then set aside until needed.

Meanwhile, heat the oil in a saucepan over a medium heat. Add half the meat chunks, if using, and sear until lightly browned. Add the onion, mix together and fry for about 4–5 minutes. Add the tomato purée and stir with the onions.

Add the Tarasaz, melon, if using, chickpeas, lentils, black eye beans and 3 litres/quarts water. Bring to the boil, then once it starts to bubble, turn the heat down and cover to slow cook, stirring occasionally to prevent burning or drying out.

After 45 minutes, add the nuts, dried fruit and beetroot, mix together, then cover the pan and simmer for about 30 minutes until the pulses are tender and the fruits are soft. Once the raisins start floating to the surface and the sauce is thick, not watery, it should be ready.

Meanwhile, make the crispy onions for the garnish. Melt the butter and oil in a frying pan/skillet over a medium heat. Add the

onions and fry slowly for 10–15 minutes until crispy and caramelized.

To serve this dish, pour the soup into a shallow bowl, then top with the roasted pumpkin, crispy onions, toasted almonds and fresh cranberries. Enjoy on its own or with breads.

NOTES

- *You can add any dried fruit, pulses or nuts to this soup – feel free to play around with the flavours.*
- *If your Tarasaz is not sour enough, you can add the juice of half a lemon or add more cranberries.*
- *We chop up melon skin and dry it in the sun for use during the winter months – it adds a nice sweet smell and taste to this dish.*
- *If you're using sun-dried Tarasaz (1 ball of Trxêna), you will need to break it up, wash it, then soak it in 360 ml/1½ cups water for 30 minutes before using.*
- *The longer this soup cooks for, the tastier it becomes as the fruit and nuts release their flavour.*

Niskêna

RED LENTIL SOUP

This is a simple yet rich and flavourful soup that's a staple in Kurdish cuisine. It's a traditional dish that we have almost every day, which is served alongside Kurdish favourites such as Shifta (see page 43). During the holy month of Ramadan, this is a core dish, usually prepared for Berbang (Iftar), the sunset feast. It's a perfectly nourishing dish to break fast with after a long day.

- 3 tablespoons olive oil
- 1 small onion, peeled and finely diced
- 250 g/1⅓ cups red split lentils, washed and drained
- 50 g/¼ cup short-grain rice
- 2 garlic cloves, crushed/minced
- 1 tablespoon dried mixed herbs
- 1 teaspoon ground turmeric
- 4 pieces of garlic bread (optional)
- chilli oil, for drizzling
- salt and freshly ground black pepper
- fresh coriander/cilantro or parsley, to garnish (optional)

SERVES 4–6

Heat the olive oil in a saucepan over a medium heat. Add the diced onion and cook for 5–10 minutes until golden brown.

Add the red split lentil and rice and mix together. Add 2 litres/8 cups water, the garlic and dried mixed herbs and season with salt and pepper. Cover and cook for up to 1 hour, stirring occasionally so it doesn't stick to the pan.

Once the lentils are cooked, the texture will become creamy. Taste and adjust the seasoning if needed. Add the turmeric last for a vibrant colour.

Serve with garlic bread and a drizzle of chilli oil, garnish with fresh coriander or parsley, if using.

NOTES

- *I always make sure to wash red lentils thoroughly to clean away any dust particles before cooking. Wash under cold running water in a fine-mesh sieve/strainer and drain thoroughly before using.*
- *Split red lentils cook quicker than the round red lentils, so it should take about 45 minutes, as opposed to 1 hour or longer for the round lentils.*

Mashêna

ماشێنه

MUNG BEAN & BARLEY SOUP TOPPED WITH POACHED EGG

Mashena is a winter dish. Due to our diverse terrains, we have some very difficult winters, made up of around 6 months of snow and cold weather, so with that you need some energy and nutrition to sustain yourself. We would eat *mashena* with *tegusheen* (bread), *nani tiri* and add lots of fried onions, whole wheat and mung beans, which keeps you full for longer, plus lots of black pepper for added warmth.

200 g/7 oz. mung beans, soaked for 1 hour, washed and drained
2 onions, peeled and diced
90 g/3 oz. barley or wheat berries
1 tablespoon sunflower oil
½ teaspoon ground turmeric
4 eggs
1 tablespoon dried mint
salt and freshly ground black pepper
toasted bread or garlic bread or Nani tiri (see page 146), to serve (optional)

SERVES 4

In a large pan, heat the sunflower oil and fry the onions for 4–10 minutes until starting to brown. Set aside some fried onions for the garnish.

Add 1.5 litres/6 cups water to the fried onions, then add the soaked mung beans and barley or wheat berries to the saucepan. Season generously with salt and pepper and taste, adjust the seasoning as needed. Bring to the boil and gently simmer for 45 minutes.

Once the wheat berries have softened, add the turmeric and ensure the soup has thickened.

Bring a separate saucepan of water to the boil, then reduce the heat to a gentle simmer.

Break one egg at a time into a small bowl and slide the egg gently into the simmering water. Cook for 2–4 minutes until the whites are set and the yolk is done to your preference. Remove the eggs from the pan with a large spoon and set aside.

Heat the olive oil in a frying pan/skillet until warm, add the sautéed onions and the dried mint, mix together, making sure it doesn't burn, until warmed through, then turn off the heat.

Take the soup off the heat and spoon into serving bowls, place a poached eggs on top and garnish with the reserved fried onions and mint mixture and a grinding of black pepper.

Serve with toasted bread or garlic bread or Nani tiri, if using.

NOTE *Back home we don't serve this with a poached egg, but I like it this way because it adds a creaminess to the dish.*

Dowkuliw be punga

دۆکلیو بە پونگە

YOGURT SOUP

Across Kurdistan, a special yogurt soup connects our people. Made with sheep yogurt, fresh herbs like mint and spearmint, and spring water. It's a dish for renewal that lasts through the summer. The fresh herbs, especially mint and spearmint, are central to this seasonal dish. In North Kurdistan, it's a cold dish called *mehir*, often served with crushed ice during Ramadan's Berbang (Iftar) for a refreshing break from fasting. When served hot in other regions during spring months, it's known as *dowkuliw*, offering comfort. Whether hot or cold, this soup reflects our bond with the seasons, the land and our traditions, embodying the simple beauty of Kurdish culture.

3 tablespoons olive oil
2 large onions – 1 diced and 1 thinly sliced
½ bunch of fresh mint, finely chopped
½ bunch of fresh spearmint, finely chopped (or use all mint)
bunch of spring onions/scallions, chopped
50 g/¼ cup barley, cooked in boiling water for about 30 minutes
30 g/2 tablespoons short-grain rice
40 g/¼ cup part-cooked chickpeas (see page 67 for cooking instructions)
½ teaspoon salt
1 tablespoon freshly ground black pepper
1 tablespoon butter
500 g/2⅓ cups plain/natural yogurt
1 egg

SERVES 4

Heat 1 tablespoon of the oil in a saucepan over a medium heat. Add the diced onion and cook for 5–10 minutes until tender. Add the fresh herbs and spring onions, but reserve 2 tablespoons of the chopped mint for later. Sauté for 5 minutes until it becomes fragrant, then add 1.5 litres/6 cups water, along with the cooked barley, rice, cooked chickpeas, salt and pepper and mix together. Simmer for 30 minutes, stirring occasionally to prevent burning. While the soup is simmering, take out 500 ml/2 cups of the soup water and set it aside to cool down.

Meanwhile, set a frying pan/skillet over a medium heat, add the remaining oil and the butter and, once melted, add the thinly sliced onion and fry for 5 minutes until golden brown and crispy.

Push the onions to one side, add the fresh mint sauté and cook for about 2 minutes. Add the dried mint, mix together, then remove from the heat.

Put the yogurt and egg in a bowl, mix and slowly pour in the reserved cold soup water until combined. Pour this back into the hot soup and stir until it starts bubbling again. Stir well to prevent the liquid from becoming lumpy and cook for a further 5 minutes.

Remove from the heat and serve it as a hot or cold soup. Garnish with the fried onion and mint mixture.

NOTE *You can add any fresh herbs you have to hand in this recipe.*

Hêlkaw

هێلکاو

EGG & SPLIT CHICKPEA SOUP

Hêlkaw means egg and water. This is considered a poor man's dish, due to the simplicity of the preparation and the ingredients. This was my grandad's medicine. Whenever he was sick, especially if his stomach was upset, he would ask to make *hêlkaw* with sumac, to get rid of the sickness. He would ask for a poached egg to be cooked in the sumac water to absorb all the sumac flavour into it.

We don't use meat in this dish in my family. If you told someone you had *hêlkaw* that day they would look at you like 'Is that it?', as it doesn't have meat in it and doesn't seem very satisfying. But we add all different elements to keep us fulfilled and healthy. Most areas call it *mazrowka* because of the sourness of the sumac and in our area (Qaladze) we call it *hêlkaw* or *tirshaw*. We would have scrambled eggs and poached eggs in the same dish with lots of fresh herbs, split chickpeas and lemon slices.

7 eggs
½ tablespoon plain/all-purpose flour
2 tablespoons oil
1 tablespoon butter
1 large onion, peeled and sliced
90 g/½ cup part-cooked yellow split chickpeas (see Note)
1 chilli/chile, chopped (any colour)
½ tablespoon short-grain rice
3 spring onions/scallions
1 small carrot, peeled and diced
1 small potato, peeled and diced
250 ml/1 cup vegetable stock
1½ tablespoons sumac mixed with 250 ml/1 cup water (or juice of 1 lemon)
½ teaspoon ground turmeric
½ teaspoon dried mint
½ teaspoon dried celery leaves (or dried parsley)
salt and freshly ground black pepper

TO SERVE

chopped fresh herbs (coriander/cilantro, mint, parsley, dill)
lemon slices
garlic naan bread

SERVES 4

Crack 3 of the eggs into a bowl, add the flour and a pinch of salt and mix together well.

Heat the oil and butter in a large saucepan over a medium heat. Add the onion and fry until golden brown, then push them to the side of the pan.

On the other side of the pan, pour in the beaten eggs as though you're frying an omelette. Let it cook through and become fluffy, then break up the eggs. Once broken up, mix it into the onions.

Add the split chickpeas, chilli, rice and vegetables, then add the stock and 500 ml/2 cups water, the sumac water and a little salt and stir together. Bring to the boil, then continue to cook for 15 minutes.

Once the rice and vegetables are tender, add the turmeric, ½ teaspoon each of salt and pepper and the dried herbs and cook for 2 minutes. Make sure the soup isn't too thick or thin.

Make 4 indents in the surface of the mixture and crack the 4 remaining eggs into each one and let them poach for 2 minutes with the lid on.

Garnish with fresh herbs and serve with lemon slices and garlic naan.

NOTE *To cook split chickpeas (yellow or green), place 90 g/½ cup split chickpeas in a saucepan with 360 ml/1½ cups water, bring to the boil and cook for 15–20 minutes.*

Kardu ganm

کاردو گەنم

BARLEY, CHICKPEA & KARDU SOUP

Traditionally, this soup would be made with kardu (lords-and-ladies), which you can't eat raw, as it's toxic and has to be cured and cooked before eating. You need to wear gloves to avoid any itching (just like nettles), but it can be picked and dried in the spring to be used all year if you are lucky enough to be able to forage for it. The vegetable looks like spinach, which can easily be used here instead of kardu.

- 140 g/1 cup pounded wheat, washed and soaked (or pearl barley)
- 2 litres/8 cups hot water
- 2 tablespoons olive oil
- 1 large onion, peeled and finely diced
- 500 g/1 lb. 2 oz. kardu (lords-and-ladies) or spinach, with stalks, washed and finely chopped
- 2½ tablespoons sumac, mixed with 250ml/1 cup water
- 1 tablespoon salt
- 1 teaspoon freshly ground black pepper
- 1 large carrot, peeled and finely diced
- 1 tablespoon vegetable stock (optional)
- 1 garlic clove, crushed/minced
- ½ teaspoon ground turmeric
- 1 teaspoon dried thyme
- 1 teaspoon dried black basil
- 1 teaspoon butter
- 1 teaspoon safflower petals

SERVES 4–6

Place the pounded wheat and 500 ml/2 cups of the hot water in a saucepan over a medium heat. Cook for about 20 minutes until tender.

Heat 1 tablespoon of the oil in another saucepan over a medium heat, add half the diced onion and stir-fry for 3–4 minutes. Add the kardu or spinach and mix it all together.

Sieve the sumac water (discarding the pulp) and add the liquid to the spinach, followed by the remaining hot water and the salt, black pepper, carrot and vegetable stock. Also add the cooked pounded wheat and any water that's left in the pan (no need to drain it first). Mix well, cover and cook for about 5 minutes.

Heat the remaining oil in a frying pan/skillet over a medium heat, add the remaining onion, stir to coat in the oil, then add the garlic and stir again. Add the turmeric, thyme, black basil and the butter, stir together, then add ½ teaspoon of the safflower petals.

Divide the onion and spices into two portions. Add half to the kardu or spinach and barley mixture and mix well, then cook for a few more minutes.

Serve in a sharing bowl or individual bowls and top with the remaining onion and herbs and sprinkle with the remaining safflower petals.

NOTES

- *You could use short-grain rice to make a gluten-free version.*
- *Traditionally we use wild kardu (lords-and-ladies) that we forage in big batches. These are cleaned and cured with sumac and olive oil and cooked for more than 2 hours (see page 134), then freeze it in small portion sizes for later use in the winter.*

Tamata û bamya

تەماتە و بامیە

OKRA, MEAT & TOMATO STEW

When I was a child, life was full of adventure. My siblings, friends from the street and I would head to the mound near our neighbourhood. That place was magic to us. We'd grab a piece of cardboard, climb to the top, sit down and slide all the way to the bottom – over and over again, laughing, racing and trying to outdo each other. Cuts and bruises were part of the fun. We didn't care about sore feet or scratched hands.

But when lunchtime came, we went home, sat on the floor, exhausted and dirty, and a bowl of *tamata û bamya* was placed in front of us. It always felt like punishment after so much fun. The stew was sour, hot and watery and always managed to spill on our already stinging feet. We'd cry from the pain, and my granddad, confused, would think my auntie was pinching us. But she wasn't. She and my mum had a routine – they'd go around with a bowl of cold, iced water and a towel, gently wiping and cooling our feet while we ate. It was their quiet way of comforting us.

At the time, I couldn't stand that stew. But as I grew older, *tamata û bamya* became a dish of comfort. Now, I love making it, especially with rice – and when there are leftovers, I turn them into *têgusheeni* the next day (see Note below). What I once hated, became a favourite memory, with the warmth of home.

2 tablespoons olive oil
10 g/⅓ oz. butter
400 g/14 oz. lamb meat, cut into small chunks (on the bone is better for flavour)
½ tablespoon salt
½ tablespoon pepper
500 g/1 lb. 2 oz. fresh okra (the smaller the better), tops and bottoms trimmed (or 1 bag of small frozen okra, washed)
1 tablespoon tomato purée/paste
5 garlic cloves, chopped
4 tomatoes, grated
½ teaspoon ground turmeric
2 small green chillies/chiles (left whole, or chopped if preferred)
Qibuli rice (see page 106), to serve

TO GARNISH

chopped fresh mixed herbs
lemon wedges
sliced red onion and spring onions/scallions

SERVES 4

Heat 1 tablespoon of the oil and the butter in a saucepan over a medium heat. Add the meat and cook, stirring, until golden brown. Add 1 litre/4 cups water and the salt and pepper. Cover the pan with a lid and leave to simmer for 25 minutes until the meat is tender.

Heat the remaining oil in another pan, add the okra and cook for about 5 minutes to lightly fry. Add the tomato purée, stir, then add the garlic, grated tomato, turmeric, chillies and the meat from the pan.

Pour the meat broth through a sieve/strainer and add the strained broth to the okra. Simmer for 20–30 minutes until the okra is tender but not mashed. Stir occasionally to prevent sticking.

Once the sauce has thickened and the okra is soft, check for taste and add salt if needed. If it is too thick, add some more water and let it simmer for a few more minutes. To check if the okra are cooked, scoop out one of the largest okra, and squeeze it between your fingers to see if it yields. Garnish with chopped fresh herbs and serve with Qibuli rice or as suggested below.

NOTE *To make têgusheeni, break up 2 flatbreads (soft flat bread or cracker wafer bread) with your hand and place it in a bowl. Ladle 2 scoops of the stew over the bread, and remove the bones from the meat. Serve it with a lemon wedge, sliced spring onions/scallions and red onion.*

Shley qeysi

شلەی قەیسی

SLOW-COOKED APRICOT STEW

Shley qeysi is a typical Kurdish dish we have for Jezhin (Eid). In the late night, women of the household prepare some dishes before the early morning because from 7am, you need to have your breakfast ready as you will be expecting guests. The night before all the women of the household gather, to prepare dishes such as this, as well as Qibuli kurdi (see page 106) and Kwlicha gwêz (see page 164) for dessert. You put the *qeysi* on the stove to slow cook, and in the winter time you put it on the wood stove and cook it throughout the night so that it's so flavourful in the morning and the apricot and cinnamon aroma spreads around the house.

2 large onions, sliced
300 g/10½ oz. chicken gizzards (or any part of the chicken)
200 g/7 oz. dried apricots, washed and cut in half
70 g/2½ oz. sultanas/golden raisins, washed
50 g/1¾ oz. split chickpeas, soaked for 2 hours in hot water, then rinsed and drained
2 tablespoons tomato purée/paste
1½ teaspoons salt
2 tablespoons olive oil
1 cinnamon stick
pinch of sesame seeds, to garnish (optional)

SERVES 4

Start by putting the sliced onions in a saucepan as a base layer, then add the chicken gizzards followed by the apricot, sultanas and split chickpeas. You should have five layers.

Mix the tomato purée with 1.5 litres/6 cups water and add it to the pan. Add the salt, oil and cinnamon stick, then set the pan over a low/medium heat, cover and cook for 1 hour.

Once the stew is thickened and the sultanas start floating to the top it means the stew is ready to serve. Can be served with Pilaw (see page 107) or Qibuli kurdi (see page 106) and garnished with sesame seeds.

Xwan

Every Jezhin (Eid) morning we would go to the graveyard (at around 4am) to see our loved ones who have passed away and prayed for them. When we came home, we would start to prepare the xwan – a small and low table made of wood, clay or even just a cloth (sifra) that you can easily move around and use as a tabletop. It is referred to as a xwana when bread is made on the tabletop. After you eat, neighbours, friends and family come to your house and congratulate you, and you would get money or give money or chocolate. If you are a lucky child you would get more money than you would chocolate. If you don't have Shley qeysi and Qibuli kurdi it is not Jezhin, it's just a normal day!

Shley paqlay tar

شلەی پاقلەی تەڕ

FRESH BROAD BEAN STEW

During the springtime, *paqla* (fresh green broad/fava beans) are everywhere and they are cooked and enjoyed in many different ways. This is a great example, where the *paqla* are cooked whole, including the skin. Kurdish people buy a lot of these beans in the springtime when they are fresh and delicate. They then blanch them and freeze them so they can be enjoyed all year.

This dish is perfect to make and enjoy when you're going out for a Newroz picnic. Or it can be cooked with hot water and salt and used as a side dish mezze, Xayar û mast (see page 126), Sir û mast (see page 126), which is then called *paqlay kulaw*. It is a very versatile dish and was much loved growing up.

- 350 g/12 oz. lamb meat chunks
- 1 small onion, peeled and finely chopped
- 1 tomato, chopped
- 4 garlic cloves, finely chopped
- 2 tablespoons tomato purée/paste
- ½ tablespoon chilli/chile paste
- 1 kg/2¼ lb. green broad/fava beans, cleaned and finely chopped
- Sir û mast (see page 126), to serve (optional)
- fried parsley leaves (see Note below) and dried chilli flakes/ hot red pepper flakes, to garnish
- salt and freshly ground black pepper

SERVES 4–6

Heat a frying pan/skillet over a medium-high heat. Once it's hot, add the meat and sear until golden brown.

Add the onion, tomato and garlic and mix well. Add the tomato purée and chilli paste and mix together. Turn the heat down to its lowest heat, cover and cook for about 5 minutes until the paste has fried with the meat.

Add the broad beans and 500 ml/2 cups water with some salt and pepper, mix and cover. Turn up the heat to medium-high, cook for about 30 minutes, then check if the meat and beans are tender and the sauce is reduced. Taste and adjust the seasoning if needed.

Serve it while it's hot. Spoon onto serving plates and top with Sir û mast and garnish with dried parsley and chilli flakes. This can be served with any rice dish.

NOTE *This dish can be cooked without meat for a vegetarian version.*

To make fried parsley leaves

Heat 2 tablespoons vegetable oil in a small frying pan/skillet over a high heat, add a handful of fresh flat-leaf parsley leaves and fry for 2–3 minutes until crispy. Use this to top the broad been stew, or use to garnish other soup and stews.

Shley barawi

شلەی بەراوی

MIXED VEGETABLE & LAMB STEW

This dish belongs to the smallholders or anyone who has an allotment or big garden. It may be a small green space but they will grow their own crops in small patches, such as okra, aubergine/eggplant, tomatoes etc. If it's the end of the season (autumn/fall), they will have a few crops left so they gather them all and put them together to make this wonderful dish.

- 3 tablespoons olive oil
- 300 g/10½ oz. diced lamb meat
- 1 large onion, peeled and sliced
- 1 large aubergine/eggplant, cubed (about 200 g/7 oz.)
- 1 green chilli/chile, left whole or chopped
- 2 garlic cloves, chopped
- 1 large courgette/zucchini, cubed (about 250 g/9 oz.)
- 200 g/7 oz. green beans, chopped into 2-cm/¾-inch pieces
- 1 large green (bell) pepper, deseeded and cubed
- 1½ teaspoons salt
- 1½ teaspoons freshly ground black pepper
- ½ teaspoon ground turmeric
- 1 tablespoon tomato purée/paste
- 4 tomatoes, deseeded and grated (no water)
- juice of ½ lemon

SERVES 6

Heat 1 tablespoon of the oil in a large pan over a medium heat. Add the meat and cook until seared all over and golden brown. Remove from the pan and set aside.

Add the remaining olive oil to the same pan. Add the onion and aubergine and sauté for about 5 minutes until golden brown.

Add the chilli and garlic and stir together, then add the courgette, green beans and pepper. Mix and cook for 2 minutes. Add the salt, spices and tomato purée and mix together to combine, then add the grated tomatoes and stir again.

Return the meat back to the pan, stir, cover with a lid and cook for about 10 minutes. Add 250 ml/1 cup water and the lemon juice, cover again and cook for a further 10 minutes until you have a thick stew.

Serve in a large bowl alongside Pilaw (see page 107) or a choice of your favourite Kurdish breads.

The taste of freedom

In 1991, when I went back to Kurdistan, my first time returning from Rojhelat after the uprising, we came back to Ranya to stay with my auntie, as Qaladze was deserted. It was past lunchtime and they had some leftover rice and Shley barawi and it was the most delicious dish. Every time I make this dish it is never as delicious as my auntie's on that day when we returned to our home. It was the taste of freedom and the return to my homeland.

Nokaw be parasû

نۆکاو بە پەراسوو

CHICKPEA STEW WITH LAMB RIBS

This is a very typical street food that you would find anywhere in Kurdistan. It's warm, filling and nutritious and a favourite in our culture. During the winter months, it's the most popular mezze served to accompany a celebratory night of drinking or as an early morning street food with *samun* bread. It's as common as serving peanuts and olives alongside drinks elsewhere around the world.

2 tablespoons olive oil
500 g/1 lb. 2 oz. lamb short ribs
1 large onion, peeled and sliced
500 g/3½ cups part-cooked chickpeas (see Note below)
1 small hot green chilli/chile, deseeded and diced
2 litres/8 cups hot water
¼ teaspoon freshly ground black pepper
¼ teaspoon ground cumin
¼ teaspoon ground turmeric
¼ teaspoon cornflour/cornstarch
2–3 thin lemon slices
½ tablespoon dried oregano
½ teaspoon salt

TO SERVE
chopped fresh parsley
black sesame seeds
lemon wedges
Kulêra zard (see page 147)

SERVES 4

Heat the oil in a large saucepan over a medium heat, add the lamb ribs and sear them on all sides until golden brown all over. Remove from the pan and set aside.

Add the onion to the same pan and fry for 3–5 minutes until softened. Remove half the onions and set aside.

Return the ribs back to the pan and add the cooked chickpeas and the chilli, followed by the hot water. Cover and cook over a medium heat for 40 minutes.

Check if the ribs are cooked and there is enough liquid in the pan. If they are cooked, remove about 1 cup of the chickpeas with some liquid and add the black pepper, cumin, turmeric and cornflour and stir together. Use an electric hand blender to blend until smooth, then pour it back into the large pan, mix and cook for a further 10 minutes.

Add the reserved fried onions, lemon slices, oregano and salt and cook for about 10 minutes to a nice smooth stew. Taste and add more salt and pepper if needed.

Place in a serving bowl and garnish with chopped parsley, black sesame seeds and lemon wedges and serve with Kulêra zard.

NOTE *To cook chickpeas, soak the dried chickpeas in a bowl of water overnight, then drain and cook in a saucepan of boiling water for about 20 minutes until soft and ready to use.*

Tarêh kurdi

تەرەی کوردی

SLOW-COOKED LAMB & BUTTER BEAN STEW

My first memory of this dish is from 1988 when I first visited one of my father's cousins and his wife who was from Mahabad. She cooked this beautiful dish for us on a wonderful late spring evening.

250 g/1½ cups dried butter beans, soaked overnight
3 tablespoons rapeseed oil (or any of your choice)
250 g/9 oz. lamb (can be neck or chop, it's up to you, but use meat on the bone), cut into chunks
1 onion, diced
2 tablespoons tomato purée/paste
1½ teaspoon salt
1 teaspoon ground turmeric
1 teaspoon freshly ground black pepper
1 teaspoon ground cumin
bunch of fresh coriander/cilantro, finely chopped (about 100 g/ 3½ oz.)
bunch of fresh parsley, finely chopped (about 100 g/3½ oz.)
bunch of fresh dill, finely chopped (about 100 g/3½ oz.)
½ bunch of fresh mint, finely chopped (about 50 g/1¾ oz.)
1 leek, finely chopped
100 g/2 cups spinach, chopped
2–3 crushed dried limes, deseeded (these can be found in Middle Eastern stores or use the juice of 2 lemons)

SERVES 6

Pre-cook the butter beans: pour 1.5 litres/6 cups water into a saucepan, bring to the boil, cook for 15 minutes, then turn off and cover with a lid.

Heat the oil in a saucepan over a medium heat. Add the meat to the pan once the oil is hot and sear it all over.

Once the meat has browned, add the onion and sauté for 5–10 minutes until golden brown. Add the tomato purée, the salt and the spices and cook for about 3–5 minutes until the aroma is released and everything has combined.

Add the herbs, leek and spinach and 500 ml/2 cups water to the saucepan along with the butter beans with the remaining water. Add the dried limes and stir, making sure the water covers the beans and meat.

Cover with a lid and bring it to the boil, then turn down the heat to medium-high heat. Cook for 50 minutes until the meat is tender and the sauce has reduced.

Serve it with Pilaw (see page 107) or your favourite rice and pickles.

NOTE *You can include the stalks from the herbs if they are soft.*

Goshtaw

گۆشتاو

LAMB & CHILLI STEW

This dish is usually made when we go for a picnic and make a firepit for cooking. The meat is usually grilled, and then anything left over is added to a large pot with tomatoes, onions, peppers and limes (carry it in your pocket so you don't forget). At the end of the picnic, in the evening, the pot is then placed in the middle and everyone gathers around to enjoy. You break your bread, or if there's any leftover bread you put it on a plate, and pour the *goshtaw* on top and eat with raw onion or fresh herbs or anything left over, so nothing goes to waste.

2 tablespoons sunflower oil
1 kg/2¼ lb. lamb meat (shoulder or leg, on the bone preferably), cut into chunks
1 large onion, peeled and sliced
1 large green (bell) pepper, cut chunks
3 dried limes, pierced with a knife
2 small hot green chillies/chiles
1½ tablespoons tomato purée/paste
½ tablespoon salt
½ teaspoon freshly ground black pepper
½ tablespoon paprika
2 tomatoes, cut into chunks
Nani tiri (see page 146) or other flatbread, to serve

BRAISED VEGETABLES
1 tablespoon olive oil
½ tablespoon butter
3–4 mild long green chillies/chiles
6 very small shallots, peeled
1 bunch of vine cherry tomatoes
1 sprig each of fresh thyme and oregano (or 1 teaspoon each dried)

TO GARNISH
chopped fresh herbs
raw sweet onion slices
pickled peppers

SERVE 4–6

Heat the oil in a large saucepan over a medium-high heat. Once it's hot, add the meat and sear for about 5 minutes until golden brown.

Add 2 litres/8 cups water and cook for about 20 minutes so it is half cooked. Remove any foam that comes to the surface. Strain off the broth and set aside, then return the meat to the pan.

Add the onion, pepper, limes, chillies and tomato purée to the meat and stir for a few minutes, then pour over the strained broth. Add the salt, pepper and paprika, mix, cover with a lid and cook for about 20 minutes over a medium heat until the meat becomes tender.

Add the tomatoes and cook for 5–10 minutes. The meat should be tender and falling apart and the sauce should be reduced and lightly thickened.

Remove the meat and dried limes from the pan, then use a hand blender to blend the sauce to a smooth consistency. Return the meat and limes to the pan.

Meanwhile, make the braised vegetables. Heat the oil and butter in a frying pan/skillet over a medium heat. Add the small mild chillies, shallots, cherry tomatoes, thyme, oregano, a pinch of sea salt and braise for about 4–5 minutes until golden and tender.

To serve, break the Nani tiri into bite-sized pieces in a large shallow bowl. Pour the sauce from the stew on top and then spoon the meat chunks evenly on top. Garnish with the braised vegetables and sprinkle over the mixed herbs, raw sweet onion and pickled peppers.

NOTES

- *You can use any red meat on the bone, except beef, as this will need more time to cook.*
- *You can also serve this with Qibuli kurdi (see page 106).*

Shley fasolia tar

شلەی فاسۆلیای تەڕ

GREEN BEAN STEW

This is a delicious slow-cooked green bean stew made with tomato, spices, onion and red meat or chicken. This is a spring/summer dish because of its freshness. It can be cooked without meat, but I prefer it made with chicken. It can be eaten with *patata û ron* (mashed potatoes), alongside Masi surkrawa (see page 99) or with rice and bulgur. Usually when we have a big box of chickens (we would have 15 in each box!), we would chop them all up and put the breasts and legs separately from the neck, feet, wings, ribs and liver to use for dishes like this one or for Goshtaw (see page 71). Nothing gets wasted, every part has a purpose.

1 tablespoon olive oil
½ tablespoon butter
1 large onion, peeled and thinly sliced
4 garlic cloves, diced
550 g/1 lb. 4 oz. boneless, skinless chicken thighs, cut into chunks
1½ tablespoons tomato purée/paste
300 g/10½ oz. long green beans, cleaned and chopped
1 green chilli/chile, diced
½ tablespoon salt
½ teaspoon ground turmeric
½ teaspoon ground coriander
1 teaspoon freshly ground black pepper
½ teaspoon dried chilli flakes/hot red pepper flakes
2 large tomatoes, skinned, cut to chunks
10 g/¼ oz. fresh dill

SERVES 4–6

Heat the oil and butter in a saucepan over a medium-high heat. Add the onion and garlic and cook, stirring, until soft but not brown. Add the chicken and stir well for about 5 minutes.

Add the tomato purée and mix, then add the beans and chilli and cook for a further 3 minutes, then turn down the heat and cover.

Mix in the salt, spices and 1 litre/4 cups water and simmer for about 25 minutes until the beans are tender and the chicken is cooked, stirring occasionally to prevent the beans getting too thick or catching the base of the pan. Check the seasoning and add more salt if needed

Add the tomatoes about 5 minutes before serving so the sauce can thicken. Serve alongside Pilaw (see page 107), any other rice dish or even mashed potatoes (or *patata û ron*, see below), garnished with fresh dill.

NOTES

- *This is also delicious cooked without meat for a vegetarian version.*
- Patata û ron *is part-mashed potato (kept chunky) that has been pan-fried and mixed with peppers, turmeric, black pepper and parsley.*

Ganma kûtaw

گەنمە کوتاو

CHILLI MUTTON & BARLEY STEW

This is a heavy winter dish, giving you energy for the long, cold winter days. This dish is traditionally cooked with a sheep's head, feet and chopped up tripe and slowly cooked with wheat/barley and chickpeas. When you put the head as the centrepiece it looks like it's staring and laughing at you. This dish is more popular in the villages and isn't as popular in the cities, which is a shame because it is such a good, nutritious meal that reflects the agriculture of our land and is not wasteful as we use every part of the animal. This dish is a great excuse to bring the family together as it's quite a big and elaborate dish to cook and enjoy.

1 tablespoon olive oil
700 g/1½ lb. mutton leg steak
1 large onion, peeled and diced
1 tablespoon salt
300 g/1⅔ cups pearl barley, rinsed and drained
120 g/1 cup part-cooked chickpeas (see page 67 for cooking instructions)
1 teaspoon turmeric
1 teaspoon ground cumin
1 tablespoon butter
1 tablespoon dried chilli flakes/ hot red pepper flakes (optional)

SERVES 4

Heat ½ tablespoon of the oil in a large saucepan over a medium heat. Add the mutton meat and 1 tablespoon of the diced onion and fry for 5 minutes to sear the meat.

Add 2.5 litres/quarts water and bring to the boil. Add the salt, cover the pan and simmer for about 20 minutes, removing any white foam that floats to the surface.

Add the pearl barley and chickpeas and cook for a further 20 minutes.

Meanwhile, put the remaining oil in a frying pan/skillet, add the remaining onion and sauté for 2–4 minutes. Add the turmeric and cumin, mix together, then add this to the meat and barley mixture. Check that the meat is soft and tender and the barley texture is like risotto. Remove the meat from the pan and shred it.

Wipe the frying pan clean and place over a medium heat. Add the butter and once it's melted, add the shredded meat and toss with the butter until all the meat is coated. Add the dried chilli flakes, stir well, then remove from the heat.

To serve, spoon the stew into a shallow dish, top with the spiced chilli meat and pour any of the chilli butter sauce left in the pan over the top.

NOTES

- *Any red meat can be used in place of mutton if preferred.*
- *This stew should be thick, like the consistency of risotto.*
- *Traditionally, you leave the meat in the stew, but I personally prefer to shred the mutton meat and dry it in chilli oil before serving.*

Qawarmay nok

قاورمەی نۆک

SLOW-COOKED CHICKPEAS

This dish was the taste of my childhood. My primary school was hidden on a road between the mud houses of Qaladze. Every day my school opened at 8 am so we had to get out early. The winter in Qaladze is very cold and my friends and I would make the 30-minute walk from home to school together – it seemed like such a long way because it was so cold, sometimes starting to snow before we reached school. Walking in the cold weather made us very tired, but we didn't mind because we knew when we got to school, we would get hot *samun* buns filled with hot *qawarmay nok* and boiled egg, a free school lunch for everyone. As soon as you entered the school you could smell the comforting aroma of boiled chickpeas and melting butter.

One of the caretakers, Auntie Fatima (we used to call her *pûr fatm*), came in early to school and boiled the chickpeas until they were tender, then mashed them with a large wooden spoon until half mashed and then add homemade butter (*rôni kurdi*) – not too much, but just enough. When it came to lunchtime she started serving, putting a spoonful of the *qawarma* onto warm *samon* buns and topped with diced boiled egg, making it a complete meal. You would only get chickpeas and egg if she loved you, otherwise you would only get one or the other.

This simple buttery dish was more than just food. It was our breakfast, our lunch and often the highlight of the day, especially in the winter where the cold morning air bit at our fingers and nose. This dish belongs to the Slemani province, and it's the oldest street food of the region. In the early morning the stall vendors on the street would offer the same meal to people on their way to work, the vendors served the warm *qawarma* with warm bread and diced fresh leek. It was – and still is – one of the oldest and most beloved street foods in Slemani and Kurdistan.

4 tablespoons olive oil
1 large onion, peeled and diced
2 garlic cloves, crushed/minced
½ teaspoon ground turmeric
½ teaspoon ground cumin
½ tablespoon Kurdish chilli flakes
500 g/3½ cups part-cooked chickpeas (see page 67 for cooking instructions)
20 g/4 teaspoons butter
juice of 1 lemon
125 ml/½ cup chickpea broth (from cooking the chickpeas)
handful of coriander/cilantro, finely chopped (for mix and garnish)
handful of chives, finely chopped (for mix and garnish)
salt and freshly ground black pepper

FOR THE LEEKS

1 tablespoon butter
handful of baby leeks, chopped (green part, keep the white part for later)
1 tablespoon olive oil
¼ garlic clove, crushed/minced

GREEN CHILLI SAUCE

1 tablespoon pickled qazwan (or capers)
2 small green chillies/chiles
1 baby leek, green part only
5 vine leaves (to give sharp fruity taste)
2 garlic cloves
juice of ¼ lemon
½ teaspoon salt
1 tablespoon olive oil

Recipe continued overleaf and pictured on page 77 ››

TO SERVE

4–6 small buns or mini flatbread wraps (or use softened Nana tiri, page 146)

1 tomato, diced

4–6 fried or boiled eggs

pickled chilli gherkin slices

roasted and salted chickpeas

SERVES 4–6

Prepare the green chilli sauce by placing all the ingredients in a blender and blitzing to a smooth sauce.

Heat the olive oil in a large frying pan/skillet over a medium-high heat. Add the onion and garlic and fry for 3–5 minutes until soft. Add all the spices and sauté together for 3–5 minutes.

Add the chickpeas and butter and mix together with a wooden spoon. Mash the chickpeas with the back of the spoon, add the lemon juice and broth, season with salt and pepper, turn down to a low heat and cook slowly for about 20 minutes.

For the leeks, melt the butter in a frying pan, add the white part of the leek with the oil and garlic and braise the leeks until golden brown, then remove.

Just before you turn off the heat for the chickpea mixture, add the coriander and chives (leave some aside for garnishing), then remove from the heat.

Serve the dish hot in individual bowls or on a large sharing plate. Place a couple of pieces of Nana tiri in each bowl, add a couple of spoonfuls of the slow-cooked chickpeas and top it with diced tomatoes with a pinch of sea salt, the pan-roasted leeks and a fried egg on top.

Drizzle over the green chilli, adding a fresh sharp contrast to the buttery mashed chickpeas. Garnish with the remaining fresh herbs and more green chilli sauce, a bowl of sliced pickled gherkins and chilli, some roasted salted chickpeas and extra Nani tiri.

Frujaw

فروجاو

CHICKEN & POTATO STEW

Usually this dish is cooked for a summer time lunch or sometimes when your mum needs a quick, simple mid-week meal to feed the family! One of the most delicious and popular dishes, it is easy to make and affordable.

- 3 tablespoons olive oil
- 1 whole baby chicken, cut into 4 pieces with skin on for flavour
- 1 large onion, peeled and sliced
- 1 litre/4 cups hot water
- ½ tablespoon salt
- ½ tablespoon freshly ground black pepper
- 1 large potato, peeled and diced (small chunks)
- 75 g/scant ½ cup part-cooked split yellow chickpeas (see page 55 for cooking instructions)
- 1 bay leaf (fresh or dried)
- ½ teaspoon ground turmeric
- 1 teaspoon dried parsley
- 1 small green chilli/chile
- ½ lemon, cut into 3 thin slices
- handful of chopped fresh parsley

SERVES 4

Heat the oil in a non-stick saucepan over a medium heat until it gets hot. Place the chicken in the pan, skin side down, and sear until the chicken skin is golden. Turn it over and let it cook in its own fat with the sliced onion for flavour for about 5 minutes.

Pour over the hot water, add the salt and pepper, potatoes, split chickpeas, bay leaf, turmeric and dried parsley and simmer for about 30 minutes over a medium heat until the chicken and potatoes are tender and the sauce has thickened.

Add the lemon slices 5 minutes before serving for it to taste fresh – it will give the dish a zestiness.

Garnish with fresh chopped parsley and serve it with Pilaw (see page 107) or flatbread and fresh salad.

NOTE *You can remove the chicken skin before serving if preferred.*

Unexpected guests

Once, when I was 13 years old, I was at home studying for an exam the next day, while everyone else except my grandad was at a wedding. We were at home when unexpectedly we had guests come round. My grandad frantically ran to me and asked for me to cook something for them while he kept the guests busy. We had all the ingredients for yapraxi bahara *(see page 35) and* frujaw *so I decided to give it a go. My grandad said he would help me, but he had no clue either. He kept running back and forth from the living room to the kitchen, trying to help, making tea while also trying to host the guests. I ended up leaving the yaprax to cook for too long until it all burned. I added too much water to the rice so it was really mushy and the frujaw was too watery. Everyone was nodding saying it was nice, but we all knew it was awful. Even though the cooking didn't end well, it's a favourite memory of time with my grandad. And I've since learned how to perfect this delicious recipe!*

Skillets, grills & oven-bakes

Lula kebab

لوله کەباب

LAMB KEBABS

The Kurdish kebab/kabob is really soft on the inside, crispy on the outside and tender. It should be cooked over hot charcoal whenever possible for the best flavour. It should fall apart in your fingers, before it reaches your mouth. There is a saying that if you can pick it up in one piece, it is not a kebab, it is elastic, you can throw it away and it will stick to the ceiling. When villagers would visit the city where there was a kebab shop, they would visit the shop to enjoy a kebab and catch the smell of the smoke of the kebab. When they returned to the village, people would know they'd eaten a kebab. The smell was instantly recognizable!

Kurdish kebabs are always made with fresh meat, as frozen meat loses its texture and taste. The ratio of lean red meat to fat is also important, with fat from lambs' or sheeps' tails being the best type of fat for kebabs.

Do not use knives and forks to eat this kebab. Take bite-size pieces of bread, place a piece of the kebab inside, followed by the grilled tomato and onion and a sprinkle of sumac, a squeeze of the grilled lemon or a drizzle of sauce. Every bite will take you on a rollercoaster ride through all the textures and flavours – smoky, crispy, soft and tender. The sweet and sour of onions and tomatoes, the tangy and zesty sumac and lemon, and the freshness of parsley, while you sip on the fresh herby *Mastaw*.

Our famous Slemani poet Pîramêrd (who died in 1950) wrote many famous poems showing his love for these Slemani kebabs, such as this extract:

Jiyani êma ka baa bê
Bo min nay gormawa ba kebabê.

This roughly translates to 'My life is like the wind, coming and going. Why I don't change it for a kebab.' We interpret this as meaning that life is short, so why waste time not enjoying the good things in life! *Pictured on pages 80–81.*

300 g/10½ oz. lamb flank (lower part of the animal, which is the top layer of ribs)
700 g/1½ lb. lamb leg meat
1 large tomato, deseeded and grated (no water)
1 small hot chilli/chile, diced
½ tablespoon salt (to taste)
2 tomatoes, cut into wedges
1 onion, cut to wedges
2 mild long green peppers, chopped
1 lemon, cut into wedges
1 tablespoon olive oil

TO SERVE
4 Nani tiri, softened (see page 146) or any flatbread
1 tablespoon sumac
Zalatay tirsha piyaz (see page 142)
1 plate of fresh herbs
1 plate of pickles of your choice
Vine leaf and qazwan sauce (see page 15) or your favourite hot sauce
Mastaw (see page 160)

meat mincer

8 x flat metal kebab/kabob skewers, 5 cm/2 inches wide

SERVES 4

Preheat the oven to 250°C/475°F/gas 9.

Cut the meat into small chunks and place in a bowl. Add the grated tomato, diced chilli and salt mix together, then push the mixture through a meat mincer and mince the meat on a medium grind plate (you can ask your butcher to do this for you if you do not have a mincer, then add the tomato, chilli and salt at home).

Once the mince is done, use your fingertips to mix the mince for 2–3 minutes until combined. Divide the mince into 8 equally sized meatballs and place on a lined baking sheet.

Have a bowl of warm water close to hand. Wet your hands, shaking off any excess water, this makes shaping the kebabs around the skewer easier. It also makes the kebabs more moist inside and crispy outside.

Pierce a meatball through the middle with a kebab skewer and start to shape the kebab around the skewer by gently working the mixture upwards, flattening it around the skewer. Turn the skewer over and work the mixture downwards, using your thumb and index finger to squeeze the meat into a long even line around the skewer. The key here is to knead the mixture onto the skewers gently to avoid over-working the meat.

Start giving the kebab 'bites' by pressing down softly with your thumb and index finger to pinch indentations about halfway into the mince. If your skewers are too long for your own, slowly try to pull it out without breaking the kebab shape, otherwise leave it in place for cooking. Repeat until you have used up all the meat.

Place the tomato wedges, onion, peppers and lemon wedges around the kebabs on the baking sheet. Season with salt and pepper, drizzle the olive oil on the vegetables and bake in the preheated oven for 20–30 minutes. Keep an eye on the kebabs as they cook, they are ready when they start sizzling and are golden brown outside but are still moist inside and the vegetables are grilled.

Place a flat bread on a serving plate. Put the kebab in the middle and the grilled vegetables around. Put the sumac next to the kebab with the salad, then cover with bread on top to help the kebab rest and maintain moisture.

NOTES

- *The metal kebab skewers can be bought from any Middle Eastern grocery stores.*
- *The best taste is made when the kebab is cooked over a hot charcoal grill. It makes it more smoky, with crisper edges and will be more succulent, although you can cook it in an oven (like the ones pictured on the previous page and as instructed here). We always use a charcoal grill in our restaurant.*

Gipay mreeshk

گیپەی مریشک

CHICKEN STUFFED WITH SPICY RICE & NUTS

This dish is suitable for any occasion, especially Christmas or any festive gathering.

½ teaspoon ground cinnamon (or cinnamon stick)
½ teaspoon ground cloves
½ teaspoon freshly ground black pepper
½ teaspoon ground allspice
½ teaspoon ground turmeric
½ teaspoon coriander seeds
1 tablespoon salt
150 g/¾ cup basmati rice, washed and drained
4 tablespoons rapeseed oil
30 g/¼ cup almonds, blanched and skinned
35 g/¼ cup walnuts
30 g/¼ cup raisins
1 medium whole chicken
1 large potato, sliced
1 large onion, peeled and sliced
1 tomato, sliced

GLAZE

½ teaspoon tomato purée/paste
½ teaspoon chilli/chile paste
½ teaspoon pomegranate molasses
½ tablespoon olive oil
2 tablespoons water
¼ teaspoon ground turmeric

TO GARNISH

chopped fresh parsley
pomegranate seeds

SERVES 4

Preheat the oven to 200°C/400°FgGas 6.

Mix all of the ingredients for the glaze together in a bowl and set aside.

Grind the cinnamon, cloves, black pepper, allspice, turmeric and coriander seeds in a grinder to a fine mix.

Pour 500 ml/2 cups water into a saucepan, set over a medium-high heat and add ½ tablespoon of the salt and the rice. Bring to the boil and cooking according to the instructions on page 107 (for cooking pilaw), drain and leave to rest in the colander.

Heat half the oil in a frying pan/skillet over a medium-high heat and cook the blanched almonds for 5 minutes until lightly golden. Add the walnuts and raisins and stir-fry for 2 minutes, then add the ground spices, reserving ½ teaspoon to use later) and mix well.

Put the cooked rice in a mixing bowl, stir in the nuts and spices to combine. Use this to stuff the chicken, then close the cavity with a cocktail stick/toothpick.

Heat the remaining oil in a large pan, fry the chicken, turning it over as it sears for about 5 minutes until all sides are golden brown. Add 500 ml/ 2 cups water, bring to the boil and cook for 15 minutes.

Layer the sliced potato and onion in an ovenproof baking dish.

Sprinkle the reserved spices over the chicken broth and add 1 teaspoon of the glaze. Mix well, then pour the liquid over the potatoes and onion. Place the chicken in the baking dish in the middle of the vegetables, and arrange the sliced tomatoes around the chicken and on top of the vegetables.

Cover and bake in the preheated oven for about 20 minutes. Brush the glaze over the chicken and bake for a further 15 minutes until golden brown and crispy. If there's any glaze left, brush the vegetables with the sauce as it will help the vegetables become crispy as well. Check if the chicken is cooked by piercing the skin at the thickest part of the thigh to see if the juices run clear. Continue cooking for longer if needed.

Serve on a large platter, sprinkled with parsley and pomegranate seeds.

NOTE *You can use the same stuffing for your Christmas turkey.*

Quraw

قوراو

'MEAT IN THE MUD'

Quraw is known as 'meat in the mud' (with various meanings). It is cooked with lamb on a *sêl* (dome-shaped metal pan or skillet over an open fire), and then mixed with sheeps' yogurt, wild oregano, spring onion/scallion, pounded roasted sesame seeds and use it as a garnish with brown butter. It is a typical nomadic dish from the mountains.

Shepherd families usually go to the mountains to feed their livestock and during the period from the beginning of spring to the beginning of autumn/fall they come back to the villages and towns. During that time, they use the *sêl* to c ook the bread on the dome-shaped side of the pan and before they finish, the pan would be turned over to be able to cook the meat inside the dome with the yogurt from the sheep. Some parts of Kurdistan call it *berxbelsel* (the baby lamb). The word breaks down to *berx* (lamb), *ber* (underneath) and *sêl* (the pan).

In Pishdar district we call it Quraw – *qur* (mud) and *aw* (water). The mud imagery is to do with the land they are living in, at that moment. The original tradition is pounded roasted sesame seeds, as shepherd's take sesame seeds, nigella seeds, fenugreek to the mountains with them to make bread.

1½ tablespoons olive oil
1 large onion, peeled and diced
500 g/1 lb. 2 oz. lamb meat chunks on the bone
½ tablespoon dried oregano
1 tablespoon butter
3 garlic cloves, crushed/minced
bunch of spring onions/scallions
80 g/3 oz. diced top green leeks (about ½ a leek)
1 teaspoon dried chilli flakes/hot red pepper flakes
600 g/2½ cups Greek yogurt
1 egg
½ tablespoon plain/all-purpose flour
180 g/1 cup split chickpeas, soaked in warm water for 30 minutes
2 tablespoons roasted sesame seeds, ground
salt and freshly ground black pepper

SERVES 4–5

Heat ½ tablespoon of the oil in a frying pan/skillet, add 1 tablespoon of the diced onion and stir in the meat. Stir-fry for 5 minutes. Add 1.5 litres/6 cups water, ½ teaspoon each of salt and black pepper and half the oregano. Bring to the boil, then simmer over a low heat for about 25 minutes until the meat is tender.

Heat the butter and remaining oil in a deep frying pan, stir in the remaining onion and fry for a few minutes. Add the garlic and mix together. Add the spring onions and leeks, remaining oregano and the chilli flakes and stir occasionally.

In a bowl, whisk together the yogurt, egg, flour and some salt until smooth and creamy. Slowly pour in 500 ml/2 cups water and whisk together until all combined. Reserve 2 tablespoons of the spring onion mixture to use later and add the remainder to the yogurt sauce and mix well.

Gradually pour the yogurt mixture into the meat, along with the chickpeas, stirring constantly, until all combined to avoid lumps and curdling. Bring back to the boil and cook for a further 20 minutes until the meat is cooked thoroughly and the sauce thickens.

Add ½ tablespoon olive oil to the reserved onion mixture, mix and add the sesame seeds.

Pour into a large sharing bowl and garnish with the roasted sesame seeds and onion. Serve with Pilaw (see page 107) or some warm bread.

Masi brzhaw

ماسی برژاو

BAKED FISH WITH SUMAC

This is one of the easiest ways to cook fish over an open fire pit. If you're fishing for fresh fish, they should be grilled as quickly as possible for the best flavour. The uniquely Kurdish way is to cut the fish along the backbone and open it out to create a butterfly giving a larger surface area to take on all the added flavour. It should be seasoned with sumac and salt and cooked over hot charcoal to create a smoky, sour and salty taste with delicate flaky fish. You brush the fish with pomegranate molasses just before serving to avoid burning.

- 1 whole fresh sea bass weighing about 700 g/1½ lb. (ask a fishmonger to wash, clean and butterfly from the back of the fish, leaving the underside/stomach intact)
- 1 tablespoon salt
- 1 tablespoon sumac
- ½ tablespoon chilli/chile paste
- 2 tablespoons tomato purée/paste
- 1½ tablespoons pomegranate molasses, plus extra for brushing
- 2–3 tablespoons olive oil
- 2 lemons, 1 sliced and the other halved for juicing
- 1 large or 2 medium onions, peeled and thinly sliced
- 1 large or 2 medium potatoes, peeled and sliced
- 1 large or 2 medium tomatoes, thinly sliced
- 1 green or red (bell) pepper, chopped into 2-cm/¾-inch chunks
- chopped fresh parsley, to garnish

SERVES 2

Place the fish in a baking pan.

Mix ½ tablespoon of the salt and ½ tablespoon of the sumac and rub all over the fish.

Mix the remaining salt and sumac and the chilli paste, tomato purée and pomegranate molasses with the oil and lemon juice. Reserve 1 tablespoon of this mixture, then brush the rest all over the fish.

Place all the vegetables in the bowl that was used to mix the spices, and add the reserved spice mixture. Mix everything together so that the vegetables are well coated and set aside to marinate for 5–10 minutes.

Preheat the oven 190°C/375°F/gas 5.

Once marinated, place the vegetables around the fish in the baking pan. Place the sliced lemons on top of the fish and cover the baking pan with a sheet of foil. Bake the fish in the preheated oven for 40 minutes.

Remove the foil and bake for a further 15 minutes until the surface of the fish becomes golden brown.

Brush with pomegranate molasses to glaze and then serve the fish garnished with parsley, surrounded by the baked vegetables.

NOTES

- *Good-quality chilli pastes are available from most Middle Eastern grocery stores.*
- *Depending on how hot your oven runs, the fish may take longer or shorter to cook, so do check it during the cooking time.*

Basirmay bainjan

باسرمەی باینجان

PAN-FRIED TOMATO & AUBERGINE

This dish, and the one on the following page, are farmers' dishes. After a hard morning in the heat picking their crops they would come back home with fresh vegetables (aubergine/eggplants, tomatoes, onions) and cook some for a brunch. After eating the food, they would have the energy to continue to harvest in the afternoon. It's a great brunch because it is simple to make, delicious and nutritious, perfect for when you are doing hard work on the land. If neighbours around the land don't have anything else to do that day we join the farmers (*herowez*) during the harvesting.

First, prepare the tomatoes. Heat the olive oil in a cast-iron pan/skillet over a medium heat. Add the onion and garlic and fry until tender and golden. Add the tomatoes and cook until all the tomatoes have wilted and softened, then turn the heat down.

Add the tomato purée and chilli paste, mix together, then add the salt and spices and cooked chickpeas. Make sure all the ingredients are well combined, then put the lid on and turn down to a very low heat and cook for about 5 minutes.

Meanwhile, fry the aubergines and onions. Heat the oil in a separate frying pan over a medium heat. Drain the aubergines, squeezing out any excess water and dry them with paper towels. Add them to the hot pan and fry until golden brown. Transfer to paper towels to drain any excess oil. Fry the coated onion in the same pan for about 5 minutes until crispy and golden.

Remove the lid from the pan of tomatoes and add 125 ml/½ cup water, make sure it's not dry, then layer the fried aubergine nicely on top of the tomatoes, sprinkle the diced green chilli on top and cover and cook for 3–5 minutes.

Remove from the stove, drizzle the sour cream over the top and garnish with crispy onions, sumac, chilli flakes and coriander and serve with flatbreads and a dollop of sour cream or plain yogurt if liked.

TOMATOES

2 tablespoons olive oil
1 large onion, peeled and sliced
1 tablespoon crushed/minced garlic
4 tomatoes, chopped
½ tablespoon tomato purée/paste
1 teaspoon chilli/chile paste
½ tablespoon salt
½ teaspoon freshly ground black pepper
½ teaspoon ground turmeric
100 g/⅔ cup split chickpeas, part-cooked (see page 55 for cooking instructions)

AUBERGINES/EGGPLANT

½ tablespoon sunflower oil
2 large aubergines/eggplants, half peeled, cut into 4 slices and soaked in cold water and salt for 10 minutes
1 small onion, peeled, sliced and coated with cornflour/cornstarch
1 large mild green chilli/chile, diced

TO GARNISH/SERVE

sour cream
crispy onions (see page 46)
sumac
dried chilli flakes/hot red pepper flakes
fresh coriander/cilantro, chopped
flatbread

SERVES 4

Basirma be tirsh

بسرمه به ترش

PAN-FRIED CHICKEN & AUBERGINE

This was my great auntie's favourite dish – she was well known within the family for this particular recipe, and also for checking every single piece of okra in Tamata û bamya (see page 59), to check each one is cooked perfectly. We would usually just serve this with bread, but it is also lovely served with Pilaw (see page 107).

1½ tablespoons sumac, plus extra to garnish
1½ tablespoons olive oil
300 g/10½ oz. boneless chicken thighs, diced
2 garlic cloves, crushed/minced
1 large onion, peeled and sliced
2 aubergines/eggplants, top removed and cut into wedges (see Note below)
90 g/½ cup split chickpeas, part-cooked (see page 55 for cooking instructions)
½ tablespoon salt
1 tablespoon butter
1 red chilli/chile, diced
1 teaspoon freshly ground black pepper
½ teaspoon ground turmeric
1 teaspoon curry powder
½ tablespoon dried black basil leaves

TO GARNISH
handful of chopped parsley
1 teaspoon sesame seeds
1 teaspoon sumac
1 teaspoon safflower petals
chopped fresh herbs
green salad
pickled long mild green chillies/chiles
Nani tiri (see page 146)

SERVES 4

Mix the sumac with 480 ml/2 cups water in a bowl and leave to soak for 15 minutes until the colour and flavours are infused into the water.

Heat ½ tablespoon of the oil in a large pan over a medium heat. Once hot, add the chicken, garlic and a few onion slices and stir-fry for about 5 minutes. Add the aubergine and slowly stir it into the chicken, then add the cooked split chickpeas and salt.

Strain the sumac water, discard the pulp and pour the sumac water over the chicken, cover and simmer for 10 minutes.

Heat the remaining oil and the butter in a frying pan/skillet over a medium heat. Add the remaining sliced onion and the chilli and stir-fry for about 5 minutes until tender. Add all the spices and mix together until the onions are golden brown. Spoon this over the meat and aubergine, stir it together slowly and cook for a further 10 minutes.

Serve on long platters, sprinkled with parsley, sesame seeds, sumac and some safflower petals and serve alongside plenty of fresh herbs, green salad, pickled long mild green chillies and soft Nani tiri.

NOTES

- *Sprinkle 1 teaspoon salt and the juice of ½ lemon over the aubergine once diced to prevent it going brown while you prepare the rest of the ingredients.*
- *You can make a vegan version by cooking this dish without the chicken.*

Silqi surkrawa

سڵقی سورکراوە

PAN-FRIED SWISS CHARD WITH POACHED EGGS

Silqi surkrawa has a special place in my heart, as it was one of the first introductions to Kurdish food in the kiosk I ran in London. It is perfect for lunch, used as a side dish or as a wrap filling, which is how I used it years ago when I started my sandwich street food kiosk.

Heat the oil in a frying pan/skillet over a medium heat. Once hot, add the onion and fry until golden brown. Add the tomato and fry with the onion until softened, then add the salt and all the spices and mix together.

Add the butter and once melted, add the Swiss chard and mix well. Cook for 5 minutes, then taste and adjust the seasoning if needed, making sure the water has reduced.

Place on a serving plate, garnish with roasted mixed seeds, sumac and pomegranate seeds, this will add a slightly tart flavour to the dish. Finish off with a sprinkle of fried sliced garlic served with a poached egg alongside flatbread.

NOTE *We also sometimes use scrambled eggs to serve with the Swiss chard in a flatbread, so feel free to use your favourite type of egg.*

1 tablespoon olive oil
1 large onion, peeled and sliced
1 large tomato, chopped
1 teaspoon salt
½ teaspoon ground turmeric
1 teaspoon freshly ground black pepper
1 teaspoon dried chilli flakes/ hot red pepper flakes
1 tablespoon butter
1 kg/2¼ lb. Swiss chard, chopped and wilted

TO GARNISH
1 tablespoon roasted mixed seeds
½ teaspoon sumac
½ tablespoon pomegranate seeds
2 garlic cloves, sliced and fried until crispy

TO SERVE
4 poached eggs
flatbreads

SERVES 4

Qali gosht

قەلی گۆشت

PAN-FRIED LAMB

This simple, but very authentic Kurdish dish is the cornerstone of our Newroz (spring new year) picnic celebrations (see below). It can be adapted to whatever herbs, spices and vegetables you have to hand, but the main thing is that it is enjoyed with friends and family to hail the start of the new year.

- 1 kg/2¼ lb. lamb shoulder, fat trimmed and 100 g/3½ oz. reserved, and meat cut into small chunks
- 1 tablespoon rapeseed oil
- 1 small green chilli/chile, diced (optional)
- ½ tablespoon salt
- ½ teaspoon freshly ground black pepper
- 250 g/9 oz. cherry tomatoes, halved
- 1 long green pepper, cut into chunks
- 1 large onion, peeled and sliced

TO SERVE

- chopped fresh parsley
- warm bread
- pickled chillies/chiles

SERVES 4

Place a frying pan/skillet over a medium-high heat. Once very hot, add the lamb fat and stir until the fat has melted.

Add the oil, then add the meat and the green chilli, if using, and fry until it has browned all over. Sprinkle half the salt and black pepper over the meat and stir again.

Push the meat to the sides of the pan, then place the cherry tomatoes in the centre and fry for 3 minutes, pushing them to the sides as they cook and soften.

Place the chunks of pepper into the middle of the pan and shallow fry them, pushing them out to the sides as they cook. Do the same with the onion and fry for 5 minutes until tender.

Sprinkle fresh parsley over the top to garnish and serve in the same dish with warm bread, pickled chillies and more fresh herbs.

Sayran – picnic day

21st March is New Year's day for Kurdish people – the first day of spring (Newroz). The roads in the cities and villages are all deserted as everyone ventures out for a day of picnics. A lot of the favourite green spots fill up, so you need to leave as early as 6am to get the perfect spot to set up for the day. To mark the new beginning of life, people make new traditional clothes with a variety of colours, traditional music is played and many different dishes are cooked on open fires outdoors, one of these dishes is Qali gosht. You can grill your meat or you can make a Qali in the big open sêl griddle (a dome-shaped metal pan that is heated by a fire underneath). You dice up the meat and quickly fry it in its own fat, then make a well in the middle and add onion and tomatoes and fry them in the same fat. You can add parsley, wild herbs, salt, or anything you've brought with you for the picnic. You don't add many spices, maybe a chilli if you want, but all you need is soft bread and your hand to eat it. People gather around and eat from the same plate.

Masi surkrawa

ماسی سورکراوه

FRIED FISH WITH SUMAC

Back home we would use freshly caught carp for this dish, cut into steaks and placed in a *sabata* (basket). It would then be covered with whole sumac berries, then a cheesecloth and stones placed on top (so the water will drain) and left to marinate overnight. The next day you would shake the fish in the *sabata* to remove the berries, dust with flour and deep-fry the fish to create a flaky, crispy, salty and sour fish. We like to remove the bone and serve the fish in softened *Nani tiri parû* (see page 146) with fresh herbs.

½ tablespoon salt
2 tablespoons sumac
1 common carp fish, scaled and cut into 6 fillets (or use tilapia or any other oily white fish)
½ teaspoon garlic powder
½ teaspoon turmeric powder
½ teaspoon dried dill
½ teaspoon dried parsley
½ teaspoon paprika or sun-dried tomato powder
½ tablespoon sea salt
130 g/1 cup plain/all-purpose flour
1 litre/4 cups frying oil

TOMATO SAUCE

1 tomato, finely diced
2 garlic cloves, crushed/minced
handful of finely chopped parsley
handful of finely chopped coriander
1 small red onion, finely chopped
2 tablespoons lemon juice
1 teaspoon red wine vinegar
1 small green chilli/chile, chopped
1 teaspoon salt
½ tablespoon pomegranate molasses
1 tablespoon olive oil

TO SERVE

Nani tiri (see page 146), softened
fresh green salad
lemon wedges

SERVES 2–4

Mix the salt and sumac together and sprinkle over the carp, making sure it is all evenly coated. Line a wire rack with paper towels and place the carp on top. Cover with more paper towels and press down – this will help to absorb the water from the carp. Leave to marinate for at least 2 hours in a cool place.

Make the tomato sauce by mixing all of the ingredients together well in a bowl. Taste and adjust the seasoning if needed.

Mix all the herbs and spices together, except the sea salt.

Remove the carp from the rack and discard the paper towels. Place the fish in a bowl, sprinkle with the sea salt and let stand for 2–3 minutes.

Sprinkle all the spices over the carp and coat well.

Put the flour on a flat plate, dip the carp into the flour on both sides, make sure it is well coated and put it back on the rack and let it stand.

Heat the oil in a deep frying pan/skillet over a medium-high heat to 70–120°C/158–248°F).

Add 2 or 3 pieces of fish at a time to avoid over-crowding the pan. This will also help the fish to fry quicker and make it crispy.

Fry both sides for 3–4 minutes on each side until crispy on the outside and flaky inside.

Remove the fish from the oil and place on paper towels to drain any excess oil and repeat with the remaining pieces.

Serve with Nani tiri, green salad, the tomato sauce and lemon wedges.

NOTES

- *Depending on how thick your fish is, you may need to use a deeper pan for frying.*
- *This is also delicious served alongside Brinji sur (see page 112).*

Rice & bulgur dishes

Saawari sûr & mreeshk ba ruba hanar

ساواری سوور و مریشک به روبه هەنار

RED BULGUR WITH POMEGRANATE CHICKEN

This versatile dish is cooked in many Kurdish households. You can cook it plain with lots of fried onion, a tiny bit of turmeric and cumin, but most of the time we make it red with tomato purée/paste and a variety of spices. As *saawar* (bulgur) is a staple ingredient in Kurdish cooking, it is used in many other dishes – rice dishes, meat dishes, salads and breads. You really can't go wrong with this recipe. It can be enjoyed on its own or any leftovers can be mixed with salad for another delicious Kurdish meal. *Pictured on pages 100–101.*

POMEGRANATE CHICKEN

2 tablespoons olive oil
1 large onion, peeled and thinly sliced
1 medium chicken, cut into 4 pieces
1 tablespoon tomato purée/paste
½ tablespoon each salt and freshly ground black pepper (or to taste)
3 garlic cloves, chopped
1 large tomato, sliced
½ teaspoon ground turmeric
1 tablespoon sumac
3–4 teaspoons pomegranate molasses
pomegranate seeds, to garnish

RED BULGUR

5 tablespoons sunflower oil
1 large onion, peeled and diced
2½ tablespoons tomato purée/paste
350 g/2 cups bulgur
½ teaspoon ground turmeric
1 teaspoon dried chilli flakes/hot red pepper flakes
600 ml/2½ cups warm water
salt and freshly ground black pepper

TO SERVE

Zalatay tirsha piyaz (see page 142)

SERVES 4–6

First, prepare the pomegranate chicken. Heat the oil in a large saucepan over a medium-high heat. Add the onion, fry until golden brown, then remove from the pan with a slotted spoon and set aside.

Add the chicken pieces to the same pan and cook for about 10 minutes, turning the chicken over halfway and making sure it's seared all over.

Once it's seared, return the onions to the pan and add the tomato purée, salt and pepper, garlic, tomato, turmeric and sumac and mix well. Add the pomegranate molasses, stir well, then add 360 ml/1½ cups water and cook, covered, for 25 minutes until the chicken is tender.

Meanwhile, start on the red bulgur. Heat the oil in a large saucepan over a medium-high heat. Add the onion and cook for about 5–10 minutes until golden brown.

Add the tomato purée and continue frying for a further 1–2 minutes. Add the bulgur, stir to coat, then add the turmeric, chilli flakes, season with salt and pepper and mix well.

Add the warm water, stir and bring to the boil without the lid. This should take 20 minutes. Continue to boil until the liquid reduces to the same level as the bulgur, stir again, reduce to a low heat and cover the pan. Simmer for 5 minutes, then fluff up the bulgur with a big spoon.

Remove from the heat, place the bulgur on a serving dish, top with the chicken pieces and garnish with pomegranate seeds. Serve with the Zalatay tirsha piyaz.

Parda pilaw

پەرده پڵاو

RICE & MEAT PIE

Parda pilaw was created in Bakuri Kurdistan, but is enjoyed in Başur and other parts of the region. *Parda pilaw* roughly translates to 'rice wrapped in the curtain'. It's cooked for special occasions, parties, family gatherings and is usually made in a big deep pot, so when you flip it over it looks like a cake. People used to make *parda pilaw* in the tandor after they finished making bread. Some leftover dough would be used to line the pan, which was then filled with rice, spices and nuts, and more dough on top. The lid would be added to the pot and sealed shut with more dough to keep the air in and so it doesn't get too dry. Charcoal would be placed on the lid so that the top cooks at the same time as the bottom.

550 g/1 lb. 3 oz. lamb meat chunks, pre-cooked, plus reserved 250 ml/1 cup broth (see page 15, intro, for how to cook)
3 tablespoons olive oil
30 g/¼ cup walnuts
80 g/⅔ cup peeled almonds, blanched
40 g/¼ cup pistachios
30 g/¼ cup raisins
15 g/½ oz. diced dried apricots
80 g/3 oz. vermicelli
1 teaspoon ground allspice
1 teaspoon freshly ground black pepper
1 teaspoon ground cinnamon
½ teaspoon ground cloves
½ teaspoon ground turmeric
1½ tablespoons salt
270 g/1½ cups basmati rice, soaked for 30 minutes
1 tablespoon butter, at room temperature
1 teaspoon mixed sesame and nigella seeds
30 g/¼ cup redcurrants

DOUGH

220 g/1⅔ cups plain/all-purpose flour
½ teaspoon salt
50 g/3½ tablespoons plain yogurt
30 ml/2 tablespoons whole milk
1 egg, beaten

round baking pan (optional, any shape)

SERVES 4

First make the dough. Place the flour and salt in a bowl and combine. In a small bowl, mix the yogurt, milk and egg and whisk until well combined (reserve 1 tablespoon for later). Pour this into the flour and stir until well blended. Knead until you get a soft smooth dough and put it in a lightly oiled bowl. Cover with a clean dish towel and let stand at room temperature until you are ready to roll out.

To prepare the rice and meat, first add the meat to a frying pan/skillet and let it sear in its own liquid and fat over a low heat for 25 minutes, then remove from the pan.

Put 1 tablespoon of the oil in the frying pan and fry the walnuts, half the almonds, half the pistachios, the raisins and diced apricots, separately and very lightly, then drain well.

Use the same pan to fry the vermicelli and stir until all golden brown. Add the spices and ½ teaspoon of the salt, mix, then add the reserved broth. Lower the heat, let the vermicelli and the spices cook evenly for 5–7 minutes, then turn off the heat. Mix all the nuts and spiced vermicelli together.

To prepare the rice, add 1 litre/4 cups water and the salt to a saucepan over a medium-high heat and bring to the boil. Add the rice and cook for 5–7 minutes. When the rice begins to float to the surface it is ready. Drain the rice and set aside.

Recipe continued overleaf and pictured on page 105 ››

Spread the butter evenly on the baking pan and stick the remaining nuts on the side and the bottom, then sprinkle some sesame seeds and nigella seeds in the tin and put it in the fridge.

Preheat the oven 220°C/425°F/gas 7.

Roll out the dough to a large round flatbread about 1.5–2.5 mm/⅛ inch thick. Make sure the bread is big enough to overhang the pan with extra on the sides to cover the top of the rice. Use the rolled out dough to line the pan and let the extra hang over the edges.

Put 2 tablespoons of the olive oil in a small saucepan and heat over a medium heat.

Start layering the filling on top of the dough. Start with a thin layer of the rice, then a layer of the meat, nuts and vermicelli, then a layer of rice on the meat, then repeat the second layer of the meat, nuts and vermicelli, finishing with a final layer of rice.

Pour the hot oil over the top of the rice, then bring the edges of the dough over the top to cover the rice and remove any excess pasty. Make sure all the filling is enclosed within the pastry and brush the egg wash on the top. Bake in the preheated oven for 30–45 minutes until golden brown. Remove and let cool for 5 minutes before serving.

Flip the pie over onto a serving plate, garnish with the redcurrants and cut into thin wedges to serve.

NOTE *This dish is fit for all types of special occasions, especially Christmas.*

Qibuli kurdi

قبولّی کوردی

RICE WITH SPLIT CHICKPEAS & CARAMELIZED ONIONS

This is one of the most famous Kurdish dishes (known as *brinj ser be xêll* in Bakuri Kurdistan) and is usually cooked over an open fire to get a smoky, caramelized flavour. The flavour of the rice speaks for itself and really doesn't need anything else added to it. An authentic Kurdish qibuli is made with Kurdish clarified butter. What distinguishes this butter is that after it is made it is stored inside animal skins to preserve it and to give it a unique taste and aroma. Clarified butter and animal skin, it's a beautiful fragrance! *Qibuli* is not *qibuli* if you don't use bread to pick up the rice and eat it with your hands, so the butter drips down your hands and makes a delicious mess!

1¼ tablespoons sunflower oil
1 small white onion, peeled and diced
1 tablespoon ghee (clarified butter)
250 ml/1 cup chicken or beef broth (or use the broth from pre-cooking the mutton)
40 g/⅓ cup yellow split chickpeas, part-cooked (see page 55 for cooking method)
½ tablespoon salt
400 g/2 cups Kurdish rice (or any good-quality short-grain or Jasmine rice), soaked for 40 minutes in warm water
bread or flatbreads, to serve (optional)

TOPPING

200 g/7 oz. mutton meat, cut into small chunks and part-cooked (see page 15, intro, for how to cook), reserving 250 ml/1 cup liquid to use as a broth
½ tablespoon sunflower oil
25 g/1 oz. pistachios, plus extra to garnish
25 g/1 oz. whole almonds, blanched and peeled
25 g/1 oz. sultanas/golden raisins
Fried onions (see page 108), to serve

SERVES 4

First make the topping. Add the meat to a frying pan/skillet and let it sear in its own liquid and fat over a low heat. Remove from the pan.

Put the oil in the frying pan over a medium heat, add the pistachios and cook for about 1 minute. Remove from the oil to keep the green colour. Add the almonds and cook for 1½ minutes until golden, then add the sultanas and mix together. Add the meat to the pan, stir well and fry for 1 minute with a pinch of salt. Set aside.

Now, make the rice. Heat the oil in a large saucepan over a medium heat. Add the onion and fry until golden brown. Add the ghee and stir. Remove from the heat and carefully add 100 ml/scant ½ cup water, the broth, split chickpeas and salt. Return to the heat and bring to the boil.

Add the rice and stir to prevent it from sticking to the bottom. Once it starts bubbling, turn the heat down and slowly cook the rice, stirring, for 3–5 minutes until the water has evaporated but still has a little moisture. Then turn down the heat to the lowest setting.

Put the lid of the pan on a clean dish towel, wrap it up and then cover the rice for the final 10 minutes of cooking. This traps the steam in the pan, helping the rice to cook evenly and preventing it from drying out. This technique will give you perfectly fluffy rice, caramelized and fragrant.

After 10 minutes, use a large spoon to fluff up the rice from the sides again, cover it and let it cook for a further 3 minutes, then turn off the heat and let it rest for 2 minutes.

Fluffing the rice up once more before serving topped with the roasted nuts and meat and garnish with pistachios and fried onions. You can serve alongside Shley qeysi (see page 60), Zalatay shwani (see page 142) or Goshtaw (see page 71).

Pilaw

پلاو

BASMATI RICE WITH BINKIR BREAD

Kurdish cuisine is heavily influenced by rice and how it gets paired with different kinds of stews and sauce-based dishes. A traditional extra about this dish is that it comes with *binkir*, which is the thin nan bread that gets placed at the bottom of the pan and soaks up the oil to make it a crispy layered treat that gets eaten alongside the rice and paired dishes. Typically, the rice is garnished with delicious toasted sultanas/golden raisins. *Pictured on page 61.*

500 g/2¾ cups basmati rice
1½ teaspoons salt (or to taste)
8 tablespoons sunflower oil
1 thin Nani tiri (see page 146), sprinkled with a little water if hard
100 g/¾ cup sultanas/golden raisins, to garnish

SERVES 6

Wash the rice in a sieve/strainer under cold running water until the water runs clear.

Pour 2 litres/8 cups water into a large saucepan, add the salt and bring to the boil over a high heat. Pour the rice into the pan and bring back to the boil. Turn the heat down to medium and let it simmer for 6–8 minutes, giving it a gentle stir halfway through.

Meanwhile, put 7 tablespoons of the oil in a small saucepan and warm over a low heat.

When the rice begins to float to the surface it is ready. Drain the rice through a sieve.

Once drained, put 1 tablespoon of the oil into the large saucepan and set back over a low heat. Place the wafer bread on the base of the pan so that it covers the entire bottom of the pan.

Place the rice on top of the bread. With the handle of a wooden spoon, make 4 holes in the rice to help the rice cook more evenly.

To check the oil in the saucepan is ready, add one grain of rice, if the rice starts sizzling the oil is hot enough. Once it's ready, pour the oil evenly over the top of the rice. Add the sultanas to one side of the rice pan.

Cover the pan with greaseproof paper, replace the pan lid and turn the heat to its lowest setting. Leave to simmer for 10 minutes.

Just before serving, remove the sultanas onto a separate plate and gently fluff up the rice with a large spoon, then transfer to a serving plate or bowl. Garnish with the sultanas.

Lastly, take out the *binkir* (this is what we call the crispy Kurdish wafer bread), break it up evenly and put it on one side of the plate of rice.

Senegasir

RICE & GREEN LENTILS WITH MEATBALLS

Senegasir is a very traditional dish among Kurds from eastern Kurdistan, specifically in Mehabad, primarily prepared during the snowy winter season. This rich dish has a combination of rice, green lentils and is traditionally prepared with rabbit meat or turkey mince along with *keshk* (fermented whey), dried sheeps' yogurt, fried onions and mint. The first time I had this dish was back in January 1991 when I got married and we travelled together to Mehabad.

250 g/9 oz. minced/ground turkey
1 teaspoon salt (to taste)
1 teaspoon ground black pepper
1 teaspoon ground coriander
1 large onion, peeled and diced
4 large garlic cloves, crushed/minced
½ bunch of fresh parsley, finely chopped
Herb oil (see page 15), made with dried mint, to garnish
bread, to serve

RICE
2 tablespoons oil
1 litre/4 cups chicken stock or water
½ teaspoon turmeric powder
½ teaspoon paprika
200 g/1 cup jasmine rice, washed
100 g/¾ cup part-cooked split chickpeas (see page 55 for cooking instructions)
200 g/1¼ cups green lentils, pre-cooked with salt
2 tablespoons keshk (fermented whey)

FRIED ONIONS
1 tablespoon butter
2 tablespoons oil
1 large onion, peeled and sliced
2 garlic cloves, crushed/minced
¼ teaspoon ground turmeric
¼ teaspoon paprika

SERVES 4–6

Place the turkey, salt, black pepper, coriander, half the diced onion, half the crushed garlic and the parsley in a bowl and mix it all together. Take small amounts of the mixture, shape it into meatballs and place on a baking sheet. Cover and let them rest in the fridge.

Now cook the rice. Place the oil in a large saucepan over medium heat. Add the remaining diced onion and garlic, stir well and make sure it's not sticking to the pan. Add the chicken stock or water, turmeric and paprika. Don't add too much salt because the keshk is already salty. Stir in the rice, split chickpeas and lentils and stir well. Cover and cook for 10 minutes.

After 10 minutes, remove 250 ml/1 cup water from the rice into a bowl and add the keshk to it. Mix well, then return this mixture to the rice. Stir it to help the rice mixture thicken slightly. Make sure it's not too thick or too wet. Once the rice has softened slightly, cook it for a little longer but remove from the heat before it gets too mushy.

To make the fried onions. Melt the butter and oil in a frying pan/skillet over a medium heat. Add the onion and fry until golden brown. Add the garlic and stir in the turmeric and paprika. Once coated, remove from the pan and set aside.

Remove the meatballs from the fridge and fry them in the same pan you used for the onions. Cook until they have browned. Add 4 tablespoons water and turn the heat down to let it simmer. Return the onion back to the pan and continue cooking until the meatballs are cooked through.

To serve, put the rice in a serving bowl, place the fried onion around the edges and the meatballs in the middle. Drizzle the mint oil on top and serve with any bread you like.

NOTE *Keshk is fermented whey and can be found in most good Middle Eastern stores.*

Qibuli raash

قبوڵی ڕەش

BLACK RICE

This rice dish is usually cooked over an open fire to achieve a smoky taste and consists of sweet and sour rice cooked with pomegranate molasses and grape or date molasses topped with chunks of mutton meat, roasted almonds and sultanas/golden raisins, garnished with pomegranate seeds and pistachio flakes.

- 80 ml/⅓ cup pomegranate molasses
- 2 tablespoons date molasses
- ½ tablespoon salt
- 3 tablespoons olive oil (or sunflower oil)
- 1 small onion, peeled and finely diced
- 1 tablespoon butter
- 1½ tablespoons tomato purée/paste
- 500 g/2¾ cups long-grain rice (not basmati)
- 1 small piece of charcoal
- 1 teaspoon ghee

TOPPING

- 500 g/1 lb. 2 oz. mutton meat, cut into small chunks and pre-cooked (see page 15 for how to cook)
- ½ tablespoon olive oil
- 50 g/scant ½ cup almonds, blanched and halved
- 50 g/scant ½ cup pistachio flakes
- 40 g/⅓ cup sultanas/golden raisins
- 40 g/⅓ cup pomegranate seeds

SERVES 4–6

First prepare the topping. Put the pre-cooked meat with the reserved broth in a saucepan over a low heat and let it reheat until all the liquid has evaporated and the meat begins to fry in its own fat.

In a large bowl, add 600 ml/2½ cups water, pomegranate molasses, date molasses and salt, mix it together until all the liquid is combined.

Put a non-stick saucepan over a medium heat and add the oil. Stir in the onion and cook for 1 minute. Add the butter and tomato purée and fry for a few seconds. Add the water mixture and stir well, then bring to the boil.

Wash the rice for a few seconds in a sieve/strainer, then add it to the water and stir so the rice is evenly spread out in the pan. Stir a few times to prevent the rice sticking or becoming lumpy. Once the water has been absorbed, turn down the heat. Cover the lid with a clean dish towel and cover the rice.

Meanwhile, use heatproof tongs to hold the charcoal over a gas flame to get hot. Uncover the rice and place a small heatproof bowl or tin foil container on top of the rice, place the ghee and the hot charcoal in the heatproof bowl and cover with the lid quickly to trap the smoke. Allow the rice to smoke for about 5–15 minutes before serving. This will give it the most amazing smoky, fatty flavour.

While the rice is smoking, heat the oil for the topping in a small frying pan/skillet over a low heat. Add the almonds and stir-fry until lightly golden in colour, then add the pistachios and mix. Lastly, add the sultanas and stir quickly to avoid burning, then remove from the heat. Keep mixing them and put them in a sieve to get rid of any excess oil.

To serve, fluff up the rice with a spoon and transfer to a large serving plate. Make a little mound with the rice, spread the meat on top and top with the mixed nuts. Garnish with pomegranate seeds.

NOTES

- *If the pomegranate molasses is too sour, you can use ½ tablespoon brown sugar or add 1 more teaspoon date molasses.*
- *You can use chicken or any kind of meat if preferred.*

Brinji sûr û xurma û ron

برينجی سور و خورما و ڕۆن

RED RICE WITH FRIED DATES

This dish can go with any main dishes and can be cooked for any occasion. We call this *nani faqiri*, a poor man's dish, because you can serve it with anything. You can build up this dish with whatever is in your fridge or whatever you can afford to use.

3 tablespoons olive or sunflower oil
1 small onion, peeled and finely diced
2½ tablespoons tomato purée/paste
½ teaspoon ground turmeric
600 ml/2½ cups chicken broth or water
2 tablespoons part-cooked green or yellow split chickpeas (see page 55 for cooking instructions)
500 g/2¾ cups long-grain rice, rinsed
salt and freshly ground black pepper
sesame seeds, to garnish

DATES
½ tablespoon butter
400 g/14 oz. stoned/pitted khalas dates
1 tablespoon olive oil
2 eggs, beaten

SERVES 4–5

Heat the oil in a saucepan over a medium-high heat. Add the onion and lightly cook for 2–3 minutes. Add the tomato purée and stir-fry for a few minutes, then add the turmeric and season with some salt and black pepper.

Add the chicken broth or water and bring to the boil. Add the split chickpeas and cook for 5 minutes. Add the rice to the pan, stir well, then reduce the heat to the lowest setting, cover and simmer for 10–15 minutes until the water has evaporated.

Meanwhile, make the dates. Melt the butter in a non-stick frying pan/skillet over a medium heat, then add the dates and stir to coat in the butter. Add 1 tablespoon water to soften the dates and with the back of the spoon mash the dates until they are all cooked through. Push the dates to one side of the pan, add the oil. Add the eggs to the pan with a pinch of salt and wait for a few seconds until the eggs are becoming soft and fluffy, then use a spoon to break it up. Mix the eggs and the dates together and stir-fry them for 3 minutes, then remove from the heat.

To serve, plate the rice on one side of the plate, add the dates on the side of the rice and sprinkle with a pinch of sesame seeds to garnish.

NOTE *You can serve with any meat dish or Qawarmay gosht (see page 130). You can serve with any green salad such as Zalatay shwani (see page 142). Even with shifta and pickles or serve it alongside Masi surkrawa (see page 99).*

Gipay parasû

گیپەی پەراسوو

SPICED AROMATIC RICE STUFFED IN A LAMB RIBCAGE

Gipa (stuffed tripe) is a popular dish in Kurdistan in the winter. This particular version is for those that dislike tripe but love the process of making it and the aromatics of the spiced nutty rice. My sisters hated tripe so, as an alternative, this was a favourite amongst us growing up, with the delicate rib meat that falls apart.

STEW

1 kg/2¼ lb. lamb bones with some meat on for the broth
1 tablespoon olive oil
½ large onion, peeled and cut in half
1 large tomato, cut into 4 wedges
1 hot long green pepper
3 litres/quarts warm water
½ tablespoon salt
5 black peppercorns
5 whole cloves
1 dried bay leaf
½ teaspoon ground turmeric

GIPA

½ a lamb rib cage with fat in tact, but bones removed weighing about (1½ kg/3¼ lb.)
pinch of salt
¼ teaspoon ground turmeric
¼ teaspoon freshly ground black pepper
¼ teaspoon ground allspice
pinch of ground cloves

STUFFING

1 tablespoon olive oil
200 g/7 oz. lamb meat, cut into small dice
½ tablespoon salt
½ large onion, peeled and diced
270 g/1½ cups short-grain rice, washed
¾ teaspoon freshly ground black pepper
¼ teaspoon ground cloves
¼ teaspoon ground turmeric
¾ teaspoon ground allspice
5 whole black peppercorns
5 whole cloves
65 g/½ cup raisins, plus a few extra to garnish
65 g/½ cup blanched almonds, plus a few extra to garnish

TO GARNISH

60 g/½ cup pistachio flakes
60 g/½ cup pine nuts
chopped fresh parsley
pickled peppers
1 sweet onion
lemon wedges

needle and thread

SERVES 4–6

First, make the stew. Put a large saucepan over a medium heat. Add the lamb bones and stir in the oil. Add the onion, tomato and green pepper and mix. Add the water, salt, black peppercorns, whole cloves and the bay leaf. Bring to the boil, removing any foam that settles on the surface. Cover with a lid and leave to cook over a medium-low heat while you prepare the *gipa*.

Place the ribcage on a flat surface, remove any excess meat and cut it all to the same size and thickness. Cover the rib meat with cling film/plastic wrap and then use a heavy-based frying pan/skillet to flatten the meat as much as you can.

Mix the salt and ground spices, except the turmeric, together in a small bowl, sprinkle them over the inner part of the ribs and rub the meat all over until well coated. Fold the ribcage into a large pocket and sew the edges together with white thread, leaving a gap on one side for stuffing. Leave the thread long as you will need it for sealing and tying off later.

Next, prepare the stuffing. Heat the oil in a frying pan over a medium-high heat. Add the diced meat, stirring to prevent it sticking to the pan, then add the salt and onion and stir until all fried.

Drain the rice and put it in a large bowl. Add the fried meat and onions and stir together. Add the ground spices and whole spices, plus the raisins and almonds and mix together.

Spoon the stuffing into the pocket you have made from the ribcage, but only fill half full to allow room for the rice to swell as it cooks.

Stitch together the pocket with the thread that was left long and close the gap. Make sure the rice inside the cavity is spread out evenly, using your hands to spread it out as much as possible.

Put a large frying pan over a high heat. Once it's hot, add the stuffed *gipa*, fat side down, and sear on both sides until evenly browned. Transfer to the saucepan of stew and cook for 45 minutes, keeping an eye on it to check if it needs more water.

Check to see if the meat is soft and cooked, then pierce each side a few times with a fork and cook for 15 minutes. Once cooked through, transfer the *gipa* from the stew back into the frying pan and sear the meat again. For some added colour, brush the meat with turmeric mixed with a little oil before searing.

To finish the stew, remove the bones from the pan and pick off the meat. Use a hand blender to blend the stew, then strain and pour it back into the pan, along with the picked meat and the turmeric. Bring back to the boil, then turn off the heat.

To serve, put the *gipa* on a large plate, sitting upright with the thread showing on the top. Place the picked meat around it. Pour some of the stew over (not too much), then take out the thread and push inward from the sides so the *gipa* stays upright. Garnish with the pistachios, pine nut and raisins. Serve the stew alongside the *gipa* with pickled peppers, sliced onion and lemon wedges.

NOTE *Ask your local butcher to debone the rib cage, keeping the meat in one piece. The bones can then be used to make the stew.*

The versatility of cloves

Mexe (cloves) have incredible properties and are very special in our culture, they are heavily used in this dish to create the aromatic rice stuffing. We have many uses for them, including as natural air fresheners, to decorate apples during Newroz and to spice our foods with. They are also used to make one of the oldest forms of jewellery for Kurdish women.

An apple studded with cloves is iconic during Newroz – given as a gift to loved ones as they would last for a long time. We call them sewi mêxek rêj. *We also use cloves as a treatment for toothache by placing the clove directly on the painful tooth and leave it to heal and soothe any pain.*

Mizawra

مزەورە

SWISS CHARD, HERB & RICE STEW

This is a traditional dish that used to be served at weddings, mainly in the suburbs, villages and small towns of the Pishdar district. Community leaders agreed to make this dish the traditional wedding meal to ensure that both wealthy and poor people could afford it. This was done to prevent those who couldn't afford elaborate meat dishes from feeling inferior. However, times have moved on and these days it is not generally cooked for a wedding meal. It is a quick dish made for brunch or sometimes you might use the leftover rice and chopped up vegetables from making Yapraxi silq (see page 27). We would always use anything leftover in another dish to prevent waste.

3 tablespoons olive oil
1 large onion, peeled and finely diced
1½ tablespoons tomato purée/paste
80 g/1½ cup fresh parsley, chopped
100 g/2 cups fresh mint, chopped
100 g/2 cups fresh dill, chopped
bunch of Swiss chard, washed and finely chopped (about 300 g/10½ oz.)
2 large tomatoes, deseeded and grated (no water)
1 teaspoon ground turmeric
2 teaspoons salt
1 teaspoon freshly ground black pepper
juice of 1 lemon
2 tablespoons pomegranate molasses
½ teaspoon dried chilli flakes/hot red pepper flakes
1 teaspoon ground cumin
2 tablespoons sumac, mixed into 120 ml/½ cup water
250 g/1⅓ cups short-grain rice, washed and drained
flatbread or naan, to serve (optional)

SERVES 4

Heat the olive oil in a frying pan/skillet over a medium-high heat, fry the onions for 5–10 minutes until golden brown.

Add the tomato purée and fry for 2–3 minutes. Add the parsley, mint, dill, Swiss chard, tomatoes, turmeric, salt, black pepper, lemon juice, chilli flakes and cumin and mix everything together well.

Drain the sumac water through a fine-mesh sieve/strainer and add the liquid to the pan, along with 1 litres/4 cups water. Bring it to the boil.

Add the rice, cover with a lid and cook for 15–20 minutes, stirring occasionally, until it becomes a thick stew with a creamy texture.

Serve with flatbread or naan.

NOTE *You can also add chicken or meatballs to this dish to make a more substantial meal if preferred.*

Pickles, ferments, sides & salads

Tirshyati kurdi

ترشیاتی کوردی

CRUNCHY PICKLED VEGETABLES

Traditionally, black grapes would be fermented for 40 days for this dish. After this time, when the fruit fly starts buzzing around the mixture, that means it's ready. It is then boiled and made into a lovely purple-coloured vinegar. For this to be a truly authentic Kurdish *tirshyat kurdi* it must have four elements – homemade vinegar, qazwan (wild pistachios), wild shallot bulbs and celery leaf and stalks. It has a beautiful aroma. Traditionally it ferments in a clay pot, with muslin/cheesecloth to cover the top. When it is served, the pickles should be placed in a bowl with a ladle of the fermented vinegar over the top to give it that pop of flavour. If you don't make your own vinegar, organic red wine vinegar works too. *Pictured on pages 118–119.*

2 small cucumbers (wild cucumber)
1 kohlrabi, peeled
150 g/5½ oz. Jerusalem artichoke, cleaned
100 g/3½ oz. carrots
100 g/3½ oz. celery stalks/ribs
½ head of cauliflower (about 200 g/7 oz.)
100 g/3½ oz. sweet heart cabbage
3 garlic cloves, peeled and halved
2 small green chillies/chiles, halved
50 g/1¾ oz. dried shallots, washed and soaked in 120 ml/½ cup warm water the day before (keep the water for later)
40 g/½ oz. qazwan (or capers), washed and soaked in 120 ml /½ cup warm water the day before (keep the water for later)
40 g/1½ oz. chopped celery leaves
30 g/1 oz. parsley, chopped

BRINE

300 ml/1¼ cups organic red wine vinegar
1 tablespoon sea salt
¼ teaspoon beetroot powder

MAKES 1 LARGE JAR

Wash all the vegetables and cut them into small chunks of the same size (the smaller the pieces, the quicker they will pickle).

Place all vegetables in a large bowl, add the garlic, chillies, dried shallots, qazwan and herbs and mix together. Sprinkle with salt and leave for 10 minutes to help the vegetables soften quicker. Pack the ingredients into a sterilized jar or airtight container.

Mix all the ingredients for the brine together in a small saucepan with 720 ml/3 cups water, plus the soaking water from the dried shallots and qazwan. Bring to the boil. Pour the hot brine over the vegetables in the jar, ensuring it covers them (the hot brine will help the vegetables pickle quicker), but don't fill all the way to the top.

Screw the lid on tightly and keep it in a cool place in the kitchen. After 3 days, open the jar, mix the pickles, and replace the lid. Within 5–7 days, the pickles will be ready to be enjoyed. Store in the fridge or somewhere cold and enjoy within 1 month.

NOTES

- *Instead of beetroot powder, you can use 1 large grated beetroot.*
- *You can use capers instead of qazwan, but you should be able to find qazwan in a Kurdish grocery store.*
- *Don't throw away the qazwan stalks – they are full of flavour so should also be added to the pickles.*
- *Dried shallots (siri ajam) can be found in Middle Eastern grocery stores.*
- *Make sure there's no oil residue on equipment; it will spoil the pickles.*

Xayar ba amba

خەیار بە عەمبە

STUFFED BABY CUCUMBER WITH AMBA SPICE

Historically, Jewish merchants who were trading on the silk road, would trade spices to the Middle East. One of the spices they brought to the region is Amba spice, made into a sauce with mango. Rather than just making the sauce with mango, as a side for shawarma or falafel, Kurdish people stuff a cucumber with herbs, garlic and qazwan, cover with the sauce and leave to pickle for 5–7 days, serving it with *kubba* (kurdish dumplings), kebabs/kabobs, shifta, sandwiches and it also goes really well with Qawarmay Gosht (see page 130).

- 240 ml/1 cup organic white wine vinegar
- 1 tablespoon salt
- 40 g/1½ oz. soft dried apricots
- ½ teaspoon ground turmeric
- 1 kg/2¼ lb. baby cucumbers, slit lengthways to make a pocket
- 1⅓ tablespoons ground fenugreek
- 1 bulb of garlic, crushed/minced
- 50 g/1 cup finely chopped parsley
- 50 g/1¾ oz. qazwan, pickled and chopped (optional, no substitute)

MAKES 1 LARGE JAR

Place 600 ml/2½ cups water in a saucepan over a medium heat with the vinegar, salt, apricots and turmeric. Bring to the boil, then add the cucumbers to blanch for 2-3 minutes. Remove the cucumbers and place on a large tray to cool.

Add the fenugreek to the pan, bring back to the boil and cook for about 5 minutes, stirring continuously. Turn off the heat, then use a handheld blender to blend the mixture for 5 minutes until smooth. Leave to cool while you stuff the cucumbers.

Mix the garlic and parsley together in a bowl and spoon into the split cucumbers to stuff. Place the cucumbers vertically in a large jar, pressed against each other, with the slits facing each other to ensure the stuffing remains in place.

To continue making the amba sauce. Blend the sauce again for a further 5-7 minutes until the sauce thickens – the fenugreek acts as a thickening agent, so the longer you blend the thicker it gets.

Pour this mixture over the cucumbers in the jar, make sure the cucumbers are completely covered and fill to the neck of the jar. Place the lid on the jar and make sure it is tightly sealed. Leave in a cold dark place out of sunlight to pickle.

After 5 days, the pickles should be ready. If the colour is still green, leave for another day or so until it turns mustard yellow. Keep refrigerated and used within 3 weeks.

NOTE *Avoid using oily and contaminated utensils when serving out of the jar. This prevents spoiling of the pickles.*

Tarasaz

تەرەساز

FERMENTED TURNIP WITH LEAVES

Growing up, when we returned from school in the afternoon, there was an old lady selling *tarasaz* every day from the beginning to the end of autumn/fall. By the time we reached the old woman's house there would be a long line of children waiting. She had a huge clay pot in front of the door, a bucket of water and more than 50 bowls and spoons. One by one she would serve us a bowl of *tarasaz*. It was so good – sour, tasty, gooey – the perfect afternoon snack. *Tarasaz* was also served outside the *hammam* (public baths), and after you'd finished bathing, you would come out to the changing area, do your hair and makeup, and there would be a lady with a large clay pot selling *tarasaz* and another clay pot with *Shêlm be trsh* (see page 125). It really helped if you were feeling a bit sick or dizzy from the heat in the hammam.

This dish is also the base for Trxêna soup (see page 46) one of the oldest traditional Kurdish soups/stews. When the *tarasaz* is sun-dried, the smell, texture and flavour changes and it is then known as *trxena*.

2 large turnips, washed and chopped into small pieces
bunch of turnip leaves (or mustard leaves), chopped
100 g/3½ oz. coarse jerish cracked wheat, washed
150 g/scant 1 cup bulgur, washed
1⅓ tablespoons sea salt
1 tablespoon sumac, mixed with 120 ml/½ cup water
500 g/2 cups yogurt

TO GARNISH
1 tablespoon butter
½ onion, peeled and sliced and caramelized (see page 46)
2 garlic cloves, crushed/minced
mustard flowers

1 large sterilized jar

SERVES 4–6

Place the turnip and leaves in a large bowl with the jerish, bulgur and salt. Strain the sumac, discarding the pulp and reserving 120 ml/½ cup water. Add the strained liquid to the turnips and mix together.

Pour the yogurt over the vegetables and mix by hand (wearing gloves if preferred) until all the ingredients are combined well. Slowly pack the mixture into a sterilized jar, screw on the lid and position the jar somewhere warm.

Every day, unscrew the lid and mix the contents with a clean wooden spoon until the mixture starts forming small bubbles and fermenting. After 3 days it should start tasting sour and you can smell the process of fermentation happening. It will take 4–6 days if stored in a warm place. Once it's ready, keep it in the fridge and use within 2 weeks.

To serve as a mezze dip, top the tarasaz with caramelized onions, garlic and browned butter and garnish with mustard flowers.

NOTES

- *You can sun-dry this, make an apple-sized ball and put it on a straw tray, cover with a net mesh and put it directly under the sun every day. Turn the balls until they are dry. Alternatively, portion the tarasaz and put in boxes or freezing bags and freeze them to be used later in the winter or just for little snacks (defrost before use).*
- *Use mustard leaves if you can't get turnip leaves, or use beetroot leaves for a pink tarasaz.*

Shêlm be tirsh

شێلم بە ترش

FERMENTED BEETROOT, TURNIP & CARROTS

I sometimes use purple carrot instead of beetroot for this ferment. It is usually made during the autumn/fall and winter months. It is another of the dishes that used to be sold outside the *hammam* (public bath). It was a welcome sight when you came out of the bathhouse. You would be hot from the steaming baths and tired from the scrubbing and the experience. You can enjoy *shêlm be tirsh* on its own as a snack, as part of a mezze spread, or with shifta, especially during autumn/fall when turnip are in season.

5 turnips, washed and bottom and top removed
3 beetroot/beet, peeled
3 carrots, peeled and sliced
5 tablespoons sea salt
1 tablespoon dried chickpeas, wrapped in a clean cloth

1 large sterilized jar

SERVES 6

Slice all the vegetables into half moons or cubes. Mix them all together in a large bowl and add the salt to the vegetables.

Put the chickpeas wrapped in the cloth in a glass jar, then add the vegetables and half fill the jar with the vegetables.

Boil 2 litres/8 cups water in a saucepan. Slowly pour it into the jar until the water just about covers the vegetables. Mix with a wooden spoon.

The water should be salty for the fermentation process, but check to see if it may need more salt, as the vegetables will absorb some.

Cover the jar with a lid and put it in a warm and dark place in the kitchen.

After 7 hours check if it has a white foam on the top and give everything a mix once more. If it doesn't have a white foam, leave it for a bit longer, check it is airtight and maybe put in a warmer dark place, to help it ferment quicker.

Within 4–6 days it will be ready to serve, paired nicely with soup but also perfect on its own.

This ferment can be kept for up to 2 weeks in the fridge – but don't keep it for too long as it is a delicacy.

Xayar û mast

خەیار و ماست

YOGURT & CUCUMBER DIP

During hot summer days, this is a refreshing lunchtime snack. It is often served topped with ice cubes on the hottest days. It's a very common and popular mezze dish and goes perfectly with grilled meats and any kind of flatbread.

2 cucumbers, grated
450 g/2 cups plain/natural yogurt
30 g/1 oz. fresh dill, washed and finely chopped (keep a pinch for garnishing)
30 g/1 oz. fresh mint, washed and finely chopped (save a pinch for garnishing)
3 garlic cloves, grated
½ teaspoon salt
1 tablespoon olive oil
juice from ½ lemon
½ tablespoon sumac
1 tablespoon salted qazwan (wild pistachio) or capers, to garnish
flatbreads, to serve

muslin/cheesecloth (optional)

SERVES 4–6

Once you have grated the cucumber, squeeze out all the excess water using your hands or a piece of muslin/cheesecloth. This is to make sure the dip isn't watery.

In a large bowl, add the yogurt, followed by the cucumber, fresh herbs, garlic and salt and mix it all together.

Serve the dip on a plate, drizzle with the olive oil and lemon juice, sprinkle with the sumac and qazwan or capers and garnish with a pinch each of the dill and mint.

Serve this dip with flatbread or serve on the side with grilled meat dishes.

Sir û mast

سیر و ماست

GARLIC YOGURT

Most of the time, this garlic yogurt would be made as part of a cold mezze. It is especially liked by the men alongside their heavy drinks. At the restaurant, we serve it as a side dish to meat dishes or Yapraxi bahara (see page 35). Ideally you should use foraged wild garlic during the springtime.

80 g/⅓ cup plain/natural yogurt
3 garlic cloves, crushed/minced
¼ teaspoon salt
1 tablespoon lemon juice
½ tablespoon dried black basil leaves, finely crushed

SERVES 2–3

Mix all the ingredients together in a bowl with 2 tablespoons water and mix until combined to a creamy sauce.

NOTE *add 10 g/¼ oz. each of very finely chopped fresh parsley, dill and mint to make a herby version.*

Dandok doyna

داندۆک دۆینە

FERMENTED YOGURT WITH CRACKED WHEAT

This is the oldest method of fermenting yogurt and wheat together to make a winter dish. It is made with sheep's yogurt and bulgur and is fermented for about 3–5 days, placed in a bowl and then dried in the sun, preserving it for the winter. You can eat it like a soup or keep it a thicker, creamier consistency and serve it as a dip. Traditionally this dish is topped with brown butter and garlic, however, I top it with roasted beef tomatoes and garlic butter or olive oil to give it more colour and provide a fresh, fruity taste. The perfect combination of fresh and fermented foods.

360 ml/1½ cups thick strained sour yogurt
1 teaspoon salt
2 tablespoons olive oil
1 small onion, peeled and diced
170 g/1 cup coarse bulgur, rinsed
1 large tomato, sliced into 4
3 garlic cloves, diced
1 tablespoon butter

SUMAC MIX
¼ teaspoon salt
¼ teaspoon sumac
½ teaspoon dried oregano
¼ teaspoon ground cumin
¼ teaspoon smoked paprika

SERVES 4–6

Put 1 cup of the yogurt in a frying pan/skillet over a very low heat, mixing with a wooden spoon or spatula. Slowly simmer until all the water has evaporated and it begins to curdle, turning like cheese, which we call *zhazhi* (see Note below).

Put the curdled mixture into a jug/pitcher and add the remaining yogurt, ½ teaspoon of the salt and 3 tablespoons water. Mix to a smooth, creamy texture.

Heat 1 tablespoon of the olive oil in a saucepan over a medium heat. Add the onion and fry for 2–3 minutes until golden brown. Add the bulgur and stir. Add the remaining ½ teaspoon salt and fry together for a minute, then add 360 ml/1½ cups water. Turn the heat down, cover, and cook for 10 minutes.

Meanwhile, heat the remaining oil in a frying pan over a medium heat. Add the sliced tomatoes and fry, turning them over in the oil until they are caramelized. Remove the tomato slices from the pan and set aside.

Add the garlic to the same pan and fry it slowly until golden brown, then return the tomatoes to the pan and add the butter.

Stir the bulgur occasionally so that it cooks evenly. Once the bulgur is cooked and soft, add the yogurt mixture to the bulgur and stir regularly until well combined and you have a risotto-like texture.

Put the bulgur in a shallow serving bowl and place the tomatoes on top. Pour the garlic butter from the pan over the tomatoes.

Mix all the ingredients for the sumac mix together in a small bowl and sprinkle this over the tomatoes to finish.

NOTE *Put the yogurt into a muslin/cheesecloth overnight or longer in the kitchen to be strained. The longer you leave it out, the more sour and fermented it becomes.*

• *An alternative way to make zhazhi, is by using keshk, which is available from Middle Eastern stores. Add 1 tablespoon keshk to 215 g/1 cup yogurt and mix together. You can make zhazhi the day before it is needed.*

Qawarmay gosht

قاورمەی گۆشت

PRESERVED SLOW-COOKED LAMB

This is a dish traditionally made during the springtime by the shepherds in the mountains, when their sheep would have been grass fed for a number of months. Before they were due to come back home, 2 or 3 of their livestock (those with the most meat and fat) would be slaughtered and slow cooked on the open fire for more than 18 hours, until all the meat falls off the bone as it cooks in its own fat and juices. The taste doesn't need any flavouring, although some shepherds might add a tiny bit of molasses or honey to get rid of the smell of the fat. The bones are removed and the meat is stuffed into the animal skin with the fat (*hyza*) to keep all the flavours inside (or a clay pot would be used). It would be placed in the coldest area with lots of snow, usually in caves or underground to help with the preserving process so that it doesn't spoil. When they return to the mountains from their shepherding, they collect the *qawarmay gosht* to take home and enjoy.

250–300 g/9–10 oz. top layer of lamb shoulder or beef fat from the outer layer, diced
1½ kg/3¼ lb. boneless lamb, cut into chunks
1 onion, diced
2 teaspoons salt
2 teaspoons freshly ground black pepper
1 tablespoon grape molasses (or date molasses)

TO SERVE
flatbreads
mixed herbs (mint, watercress, rocket/arugula)
lemon slices
pickled chillies/chiles

large sterilized jar

SERVES 4

Heat a non-stick pan over a medium-high heat until it is very hot (to smoking point), then add the diced fat. With a wooden spoon, stir very fast so it's not burning or sticking to the pan as this action will help the fat caramelize as it melts away. Add the lamb meat and stir continuously until all the meat has seared. Add the diced onion, salt and black pepper.

Mix the grape molasses with 125 ml/½ cup water and add to the pan. Turn the heat to the lowest setting, cover and simmer for about 1 hour, but occasionally check it isn't sticking to the bottom of the pan and add more salt, pepper or water if needed.

Once the meat is cooked thoroughly, it should become caramelized, soft and all the water should have reduced in the process. This will give you a very rich flavour of caramelized meat.

Transfer to a jar along with all the oil. Close the lid and keep in the fridge for up to 6 months. You can serve this dish for breakfast with eggs, on flatbreads with herbs, lemon slices and pickled chillies, add to any stews for extra flavour or serve it with nuts and raisins as a garnish for rice.

Qotan – the Kurdish fridge

Before domestic fridges, we had to make our own. Two large holes would be dug in the garden, usually just outside the kitchen, side by side, and about 2 metres/6½ feet deep and wide. The tandor would be placed in one for cooking. The other would have wooden beams placed over the hole with access left to be able to go in and retrieve items. This is the qotan, the Kurdish version of a fridge. Meat, butter, cheese and even fruit and vegetables would be kept inside for preservation.

40 OZS. (2 LBS. 8 OZS.)

Shêlmi kulaw

شێلمی کوڵاو

TURNIP COOKED IN BLACK TEA

Traditionally, this dish would be cooked overnight so the next day you can taste the rich sweetness, colour and bitterness of the turnips. You can have this as a street food and snack any time of the day, preferably after dinner (if you don't want something sweet). It's a winter warm-hearted snack, any time of the day.

Early morning in the cold winter months, as people are going to work or children go to school this is a popular street food similar to Qawarmay nok (see page 75), Paqlay surkrawar (see page 138) and Nokaw (see page 67), and is enjoyed by people of all ages and all classes. I have many memories of lining up behind all sorts of people with my friends on the way to school to buy some *shêlmi kulaw* from an elderly man with a hand cart. It would be like an ice cream truck, but instead an old man shouting with a hoarse voice '*Shêlmi Kulaw! Shêlmi Kulaw!*'

1 tablespoon loose black tea leaves
200 g date molasses
3 large turnips, washed, ends trimmed and cut in half
½ tablespoon smoked sea salt, to garnish

Kurdish teapot (qori)

SERVES 4–6

Put 500 ml/2 cups cold water into a teapot and add the black tea leaves. Place over a very low heat to brew for about 20 minutes until bubbling lightly and then turn off the heat.

Pour 1 litre/4 cups water into a large saucepan, add the date molasses and mix well. Set over a medium heat and bring to the boil. Add the turnip to the saucepan and cook for 15 minutes.

Strain the tea into the saucepan and gently mix together to avoid breaking the turnips. Simmer for 30 minutes until the turnips are tender and cooked inside – you can test this by poking the turnips with the tip of the knife. They should be soft but not mushy. If you think there is too much liquid, turn the heat up for 3–5 minutes and let it bubble until reduced, taking care not to burn the sides.

Place a turnip half inside a round bowl, slice into thin half-moons and gently press down to fan out the layers. Sprinkle some smoked sea salt on top to garnish and serve hot.

Kasa Drowsĉ – neighbour's plate

Kurdish neighbours will often share plates of food between households. This is often when you have made a dish that is lengthy or complicated to prepare, such as fermented foods, or foods, such as bread, that can be made in large batches. This is mostly practised during Ramadan as a form of charity, when households that are wealthier help their neighbours who can't afford certain dishes, such as those with meat in.

Kardui surkrawa

کاردوی سورکراوه

STIR-FRIED SPINACH OR KARDU

This dish would traditionally be cooked in the spring and made with kardu (lords-and-ladies). Kardu is a wild foraged vegetable that needs to be cured before using, due to its toxicity when raw (see below). Once cured it has the same taste and texture as spinach, so this dish will work with either option, but do seek out kardu if you can. You can find kardu in the shady areas of mountains, but you must use gloves to pick them as it will make you itchy. It is unique because when kardu is cured with sumac and olive oil, it gives it a delicious taste. It is such a versatile leafy vegetable – you can stir-fry it, add it to soups and stews, cook it with meat, or even in a rice dish (*kardu qibuli*) – the options are endless.

2 tablespoons sumac mixed with 250ml/1 cup water
1 kg/2¼ lb. fresh spinach with stalks, washed and roughly chopped (or cured kardu/ lords-and-ladies)
2 tablespoons olive oil
1 tablespoon butter
1 large onion, peeled and sliced
1 tomato, skinned and chopped
1 tablespoon salt
1 teaspoon freshly ground black pepper
juice of ½ lemon
pinch of paprika
½ teaspoon dried chilli flakes/ hot red pepper flakes
4 eggs, beaten with a pinch of salt

TO GARNISH

chopped fresh parsley
1 tablespoon mixed seeds toasted with lemon juice and pinch of salt

SERVES 4

Put a saucepan on the stove and add 250 ml/1 cup water. Strain the sumac water into the pan (discarding the pulp) and bring it to the boil.

Mix in the spinach or kardu and simmer until tender and wilted. Drain in a fine-mesh sieve/strainer and use a flat spoon to press lightly on the spinach to remove excess water.

Heat half the oil and butter in a large shallow frying pan/skillet over a medium heat, add the onion and fry until soft golden brown.

Add the tomato and fry for 3–4 minutes. Add the spinach and mix well. Add the salt and pepper and add the lemon juice. Turn down the heat while cooking.

Heat the remaining oil and butter in a separate frying pan over a medium heat and add the paprika and chilli flakes. Add the beaten eggs, keeping the mixture moving around the pan until it all becomes soft and fluffy.

While the eggs are still hot, mix half of it through the stir-fried spinach and place on a serving plate. Top with the remaining egg mixture and sprinkle with chopped parsley and roasted mixed seeds and serve with warm soft bread.

Curing kardu (lords-and-ladies)

Wash kardu in cold running water, shake or pat dry and then roughly chop. Place the kardu in a saucepan with 2 litres/8 cups water. Add 120 ml/ ½ cup sumac water (soak 1 tablespoon sumac in the water for 1 hour, then strain the liquid into the pan, discarding the sumac). Bring it to the boil and cook for 1½ hours. Add 1 tablespoon salt, the juice of 2 lemons and 2 tablespoons olive oil and cook for 30 minutes. Test if the kardu is fully cured by tasting a small amount – if it still causes a mild tingle, then it needs to be cooked for another 30 minutes. Drain before using.

Kinger masi

کنگر ماسی

FRIED KINGER PATTIES

Kinger (wild artichokes) can sometimes be found in Kurdish grocery stores during the spring months. These poached kinger patties are perfect served alongside watercress, tomatoes, cucumber, amba sauce and Mastaw (see page 160) as a fresh and delicious sharing spread.

Add 1 litre/4 cups water to a saucepan, bring it to the boil, add the salt and half the lemon juice and mix. Add the kinger (or alternative vegetable) and simmer for 10–20 minutes until tender and soft (leeks or asparagus won't need as long to cook – about 3–5 minutes). Drain the kinger and let it cool slightly.

Take 2 or more pieces of kinger and squeeze out the water with your hands, flatten them into patties and place on a baking sheet. If you are using baby leeks and/or asparagus, pierce 2 or 3 onto cocktail sticks.

In a bowl, mix the egg, black pepper, chilli flakes, mixed herbs and ¼ teaspoon salt.

Put the flour on a flat plate. Dip the kinger into the egg, then dip into the flour. Do the same for the others and put it back on the baking sheet.

Heat the oil in a frying pan/skillet over a medium-high heat. To check if the oil is hot enough, you can drop in a tiny piece of the flour coated kinger; if it starts to float, it is hot enough.

One by one, add the patties and fry for 1–2 minutes on each side. Transfer from the pan to a baking sheet lined with paper towels to drain any excess oil. Repeat until all of the patties have been fried.

Serve the fried patties with salad, sauce for dipping, flatbreads and Mastaw for the best flavour.

NOTES

You can get kinger in some Middle Eastern grocery stores during spring. If you do manage to get some, you must remove the top layer and the thorns before use. Alternatively, if you can't get hold of kinger, try using:

- *Baby leeks – (white and light green parts, if they are long), divided into 3–4 pieces, boiled in slightly salty water and lemon juice as it's a little bit sweeter than kinger.*
- *White or green asparagus – trim the ends, then cut the asparagus into the same as the leeks.*

1½ tablespoons salt
juice of 1 lemon
1 kg/2¼ lb. kinger (wild artichokes), cleaned and washed (see Notes below for alternatives)
1 large egg
½ teaspoon freshly ground black pepper
½ teaspoon dried chilli flakes/hot red pepper flakes
1 teaspoon dried mixed herbs
2½ tablespoons plain/all-purpose flour
250 ml/1 cup sunflower oil

TO SERVE (OPTIONAL)

80 g/3 oz. watercress washed
1 large tomato, sliced
1 red onion, thinly sliced
1 cucumber, cut to thin matchsticks
1 tablespoon sumac
Amba sauce or Sir û mast (see page 126)
Mastaw (see page 160)
Nani tiri (see page 146) or any flatbread

SERVES 4–6

Paqlay surkrawar

پاقلەی سورکراوە

STIR-FRIED BROAD BEANS WITH POMEGRANATE MOLASSES

Paqlay surkrawar is one of the most popular street foods in Kurdistan, cooked with lots of sumac, molasses, spices and chilli, but some prefer them plain. This is eaten by all, but is most enjoyed during a night of drinks, just like Nokaw be parasû (see page 67). Take this dish to your Newroz picnic as a simple and easy accompaniment to your *sayran* (picnic). You can serve this on top of any salad, like Zalatay tirsha piyaz (see page 142) and due to the salty, sour taste you can serve it on top of Qawarmay nok (see page 75), or alongside any meat dishes.

- 300 g/2 cups large dried broad/fava beans, soaked overnight
- 1 tablespoon salt
- 2 tablespoons olive oil
- 1 teaspoon crushed coriander seeds
- 1 tablespoon medium hot chilli/chile sauce
- 1 tablespoon sumac
- ½ tablespoon paprika
- 2 tablespoons pomegranate molasses
- pinch of salt

TO GARNISH

- 1 tablespoon very finely chopped fresh coriander
- 2 tablespoons pomegranate seeds

SERVES 4-5

Fill a large saucepan with 2 litres/quarts water, add the beans, salt and half the olive oil and bring it to the boil. Cover the pan and leave to simmer for about 1 hour (depending on the quality of the beans) until the beans are tender and soft without being mashed up. Drain the beans well.

Place a deep frying pan/skillet over a medium heat to get hot. Add the crushed coriander seeds and roast for 1 minute, then remove from the pan.

Return the pan to the heat, add the remaining olive oil, the chilli sauce, sumac, paprika, pomegranate molasses and a pinch of salt and mix well. Add the drained beans to the sauce and toss well, stirring very quickly to avoid burning. Stir well until all beans are coated with the sauce, then sprinkle the toasted coriander seeds over the top and toss together.

Place in a serving bowl, garnish with chopped coriander and pomegranate seeds and serve as a hot or cold snack.

NOTES

- *Use as a cold mezze and pair it with your favourite drinks.*
- *You can use a pressure cooker to reduce the cooking time by around 30 minutes.*
- *You can use a large plain tin of broad/fava beans.*

Zalatay kuzala

زەڵاتەی کوزەلە

WATERCRESS, RADISH & POMEGRANATE SALAD

During the picnic for Newroz, we put our food on the same *xwan* (table) and eat together. If there are any issues you have with anyone, friends or family, it is encouraged to make peace during this time. Kuzala salad is a good representation of Newroz as *kuzala* (watercress), *punga* (spearmint) and *qazwan* (wild pistachio), are all foraged items put together to make a fresh herb bowl, which is eaten alongside any dishes. Back home, you could walk down any stream from the mountain and watercress would be blooming all along the sides, that you could forage in large bunches. You can sit down with anyone during Newroz and make friends with them; we approach this celebration with openness.

80 g/1½ cups watercress, washed
3–4 radishes, tops removed and thinly sliced
1 long paprika pepper, cut into thin round slices
1 lemon, halved (one half thinly sliced and the other used for juice in the dressing)
1 large pomegranate

DRESSING

2 tablespoons qazwan (or capers)
½ teaspoon English mustard
1 tablespoon honey
juice of ½ lemon
1 tablespoon olive oil
1 teaspoon chopped fresh dill
salt

SERVES 4

Assemble the watercress, radishes, peppers and sliced half-lemon in a large bowl.

Cut the pomegranate into quarters, without cutting the whole way through to make sure it is intact. Open up the pomegranate like a flower, hold it over the bowl and beat the back of it with a spoon until all the seeds have come out. Mix all the salad ingredients in the bowl.

Mix the dressing ingredients in a small bowl and pour evenly over the salad just before serving.

NOTE *This is nice with Masi surkrawa (see page 99), Masi brzhaw (see page 88) or Shiftay gosht (see page 43).*

Xakalewa (Newroz) – celebration of the new year

Newroz is the Kurdish New Year, celebrating the start of spring. Like Christmas Eve, we have Newroz Eve on 20th March when the sun goes down until the early hours of the morning. In the weeks and days before the celebration, wood will be collected ready for the Newroz fires. Every single home goes to the roof of the house (terrace) or the front of the house and lights a fire when the sun sets and the night begins. The fire has multiple meanings, but it represents the sign of victory and the resilience of the Kurdish people. All around the town/village every house will have a fire and it will look like fairy lights from a distance. The fire is a sign of light in the darkness; it is to celebrate victory for freedom.

Zalatay tirsha piyaz

ONION SLAD

زەڵاتەی ترشە پیاز

This is one of the simplest salads, pairing perfectly with grilled kebabs/kabobs and chicken shish. It's made of tomatoes, sweet red onion, parsley and sumac. It has a lovely sour taste so works well with the Lula kebab (see page 82) in particular, as the sour taste cuts through the fat in rich meat dishes.

2 large red onions, peeled and cut into julienne/thin slices
1 large tomato, cut into julienne/thin slices
1 long green biber pepper, cut into julienne/thin slices
1 large hot biber pepper, cut into julienne/thin slices
bunch of flat-leaf celery (or parsley), washed and finely chopped
seeds from 1 pomegranate
½ tablespoon sumac
1 teaspoon salt
1 teaspoon red chilli/chile paste
juice of 1 lemon
2 tablespoons olive oil
2 tablespoons pomegranate molasses
chopped spring onions/scallions, to garnish

SERVES 4

Place the onions, tomato and peppers in a large bowl. Add half the chopped herbs and pomegranate seeds and reserve the rest to garnish.

Mix the sumac, salt, chilli paste, lemon juice, olive oil and pomegranate molasses in a separate small bowl and combine well until a thick sauce.

Pour the sauce over the vegetables and mix together. Garnish with the reserved herbs, pomegranate seeds and spring onions to finish. Serve with any grilled meat as a side dish or use with bulgur rice.

Zalatay shwani

SHEPHERD'S SALAD

زەڵاتەی شوانی

Zalatay shwani is a very popular Kurdish salad, easy to assemble and a typical spring dish once cucumbers come into season. Traditionally this salad was eaten by shepherds, along with homemade cheese, yogurt or mastaw (see page 160). The only thing they would take with them up into the mountains was a *turbên* (bag) full of food to sustain them while they watched their sheep and livestock. The bag is made from wool and is lined with animal skins cured with special nuts called *glwan*, this keeps the food cool.

2 large beef tomatoes
2 large cucumbers
1 large red onion
handful of pomegranate seeds
1 tablespoon sumac
1 teaspoon salt
1 tablespoon pomegranate molasses
1 tablespoon olive oil
½ tablespoon date molasses
1 small green chilli/chile, deseeded and finely chopped
bunch of parsley, washed and finely chopped

SERVES 4–6

Wash the vegetables and finely dice them. You want the vegetables to be the size of pomegranate seeds. Place them all in a large bowl and mix with the pomegranate seeds, reserving a little for a garnish.

Mix the sumac, salt, pomegranate molasses, olive oil, date molasses and the small chilli to create the dressing. Drizzle the dressing over the salad and toss together. Add the parsley and dill and toss again. Garnish with pomegranate seeds and more herbs (if you like).

Serve this with any meat dish, veg, kebab/kabob, or *qibuli* (rice) dish.

Breads

Nani tiri

نانی تیری

FLAT WAFER BREAD

Nani tiri is the perfect bread to use for a Newroz (spring) picnic – you can make a big batch of them and easily transport them to your picnic. This bread is dehydrated but if you splash water on it, the bread rehydrates and becomes so soft. It is perfect for using as a wrap with kebab/kabob or eating with other grilled meats. You don't need a fork or knife when you have *nani tiri*! You can also use it as a cracker for mezze dips, you can use it as *têgusheen* for Goshtaw (see page 71), Tamata û bamya (see page 59) or any type of stew, and you can make it into *paru* (small bites) for serving with stir-fries, meat or for topping salads.
Pictured on pages 144–145.

420 g/3 cups strong white flour, plus extra for dusting
½ teaspoon sea salt
1 tablespoon black sesame seeds
¼ teaspoon roasted ground fenugreek
320 ml/1⅓ cups lukewarm water

large flat non-stick skillet **(traditionally this bread is cooked on a *saj*, a large dome-shaped, convex metal griddle that is heated by a fire underneath)**

MAKES 15

Sift the flour into a large bowl, add the salt, sesame seeds and fenugreek, mix together, then push over to one side of the bowl.

Gradually add the water and slowly mix together with the flour until almost blended. Keep about 1 tablespoon of the water to wet your hands and knead the dough until it's smooth and firm, then cover with a clean dish towel and let rest for 3–5 minutes.

Sprinkle some flour on the work surface and over a baking sheet. On the floured surface, divide the dough into 15 portions (about 55 g/2 oz. each). Hold the dough in your hand, and dust it with a little flour from the work surface, shape it like a ball and place on the floured baking sheet. Repeat for the other portions, then cover to avoid them getting too dry.

Sprinkle some more flour on the work surface and roll the dough balls, one at the time, into a thin, round sheet – the thinner and flatter the sheet, the quicker the bread will cook and it will stay crisper for longer.

Place a frying pan/skillet over a medium-high heat.

Use the rolling pin to lift up one flat sheet of dough and place it in the skillet. Cook for 1–2 minutes until the dough is firm and golden, then turn it over and grill the other side. The bread should be crispy on both sides. Remove from the heat, let cool and repeat for the other flat sheets.

Stack the breads on top of each other so they retain their shape.

NOTE *As the bread is dehydrated, it will keep for up to 3 months in a dry, dark place (away from direct sunlight). The thinner the bread, the longer it will keep.*

Kulêra zard

كولێره زەرد

FLUFFY BREAD

The kaghly topping used on this fluffy bread is very common in Kurdistan and can be used on any type of bread. *Kulêra zard* is a traditional round breakfast bread and historically was stamped with the bone of a goat. Bones were cooked with dishes like *gipa* (stuffed tripe) and the head and feet of a goat for extra flavour. The bones would be placed in boiling water and cook for hours until all the meat, collagen and oil had dissolved from the bone. Specifically, the bone is called *meech* and is taken out and hung up to dry in the sun and then it is used to stamp a pattern into *kulêra zar*d using the joint on the bone as a decorative tool.

Pictured on pages 144–145.

500 g/3¾ cups strong white flour or plain/all-purpose flour, plus extra for dusting
½ tablespoon dried yeast
½ tablespoon sugar
½ tablespoon salt (as required)
360 ml/1½ cups warm water
2 tablespoons olive oil
butter, for brushing

KAGHLY TOPPING

1 egg yolk
½ tablespoon sesame seeds
½ tablespoon nigella seeds
½ tablespoon plain yogurt
1 tablespoon olive oil
½ tablespoon safflower petals, mixed with 2 tablespoons hot water

MAKES 6

First make the topping. The earlier you make kaghly, the better the taste and colour. Put all the ingredients together in a bowl and mix well. Set aside to rest for the flavours to come together.

Next, make the dough. Sift the flour into a bowl and add the yeast and sugar, mixing well, then add the salt.

Mix the water and olive oil together, then slowly pour it into the flour. Mix with your hand until you form a smooth, slightly soft dough that is not too firm or sticky. Bring it to the middle of the bowl. Wet your hand and gently rub the dough while it's resting to prevent it from drying. Cover the bowl with cling film/plastic wrap and a clean dish towel. Place in a warm spot for at least 15 minutes to rise, depending on your room temperature.

Once the dough has fully risen, take it out and place it on a floured surface. Divide it into 6 equal portions and form them into round balls. Place on a floured baking sheet, cover and leave to rise while you preheat the oven.

Preheat the oven to 250°C/475°F/gas 9 for about 20 minutes. Then, turn it down to 180°C/350°F/gas 4 once you start baking.

Take one dough ball at a time and place it on a lightly floured surface. With your hands, flatten the dough to form an even round shape, then use your fingertips to push dimple marks into the dough. Put 3–4 breads on one baking sheet lined with baking paper. Leave to rest for 3–5 minutes.

Brush the dough all over with the kaghly topping. Bake one sheet of bread at a time for about 15–20 minutes. Check if more time is needed, depending on your oven. When baked, take them out and brush butter on top to finish.

Serve with yogurt, honey, soft cream cheese, or just brewed hot, sweet cardamom black tea.

Kulêra mezhga

کولێره مژگه

BREAKFAST BREAD

One of the oldest types of Kurdish bread, especially made in the Hawraman region near the Zagros mountains in both south and east Kurdistan.

500 g/3¾ cups strong white flour
1½ teaspoons dried yeast
1 tablespoon white sugar
1½ teaspoons salt
250 ml/1 cup milk
125 ml/½ cup water
3 tablespoons sunflower oil
butter, at room temperature, for brushing

FILLING
300 g/2½ cups chopped walnuts
1 white onion, peeled and diced
pinch of salt

KAGHLY TOPPING
1 large egg yolk
½ tablespoon safflower, soaked in 2 tablespoons hot water
½ tablespoon plain/natural yogurt
1 tablespoon olive oil
½ tablespoon nigella seeds (or black sesame seeds)
½ tablespoon sesame seeds

MAKES 4–6

Preheat the oven to 180°C/350°F/gas 4.

First make the dough. In a large bowl, mix the flour, yeast and sugar, then add the salt on one side of the mixture.

Place all the wet ingredients in a separate bowl and mix together. Add this to the flour and bring everything together until you have a smooth, soft dough. It should not stick to the sides of the bowl; if it does that means the dough is too wet and you might need to add some more flour. Once it is ready, cover the bowl with a clean dish towel and let it rest for 10–15 minutes.

Divide the dough evenly into 4–6 equal portions and form them into small balls, then let it rest again for 15 minutes.

For the filling, blitz the chopped walnuts in a blender until they are finely chopped. Tip them into a bowl and add the onion and a pinch of salt and mix together.

To make the kaghly topping, place all the ingredients in a separate bowl and mix together. Set aside for the flavours to develop.

Take one dough ball and press it flat with your hand on a flat surface, making sure it is the same thickness all around. Once you have the dough flat, place 2 tablespoons of the filling in the middle, then gather the edges of the dough into the middle and close tightly to seal.

Turn the dough parcel over and use your hands to make it flat and round again. Put the flat stuffed dough onto a baking sheet and repeat for the other dough balls.

Brush the kaghly mixture evenly over the surface of the bread. Bake in the preheated oven for 20–25 minutes until nice and crispy.

Brush butter all over the bread as soon as it is taken out of the oven and serve with your favourite breakfast condiments.

Kalana

کەلانە

FLATBREAD STUFFED WITH SPRING ONIONS

Kalana is a staple stuffed bread dish in Kurdistan and served at all times of the day. Usually made in early spring when people go foraging and they bring their harvest home, which includes wild garlic, three-cornered leeks (*lusha*) and spring onions/scallions. Thus kalana is made to celebrate the arrival of spring (but is also made throughout the year). When my mother and aunt made this bread it would be served on a round wooden tray with a big bowl of sugar syrup in the middle. We would all gather round and tear off pieces of the bread and dip in the syrup for a delicious sweet treat.

360 g/2¾ cups plain/all-purpose flour, plus extra for dusting
300 ml/1¼ cups warm water
1 tablespoon olive oil
300 g/10½ oz. spring onion/scallions (or wild garlic if in season), washed and chopped
80 g/⅓ cup/¾ stick butter or rapeseed oil
date molasses or sugar syrup, to drizzle
salt

MAKES 4–6

First, make the dough by putting the flour into a large bowl with 1 teaspoon salt. Make a well in the middle and pour in the warm water slowly and mix together. Then pour in the oil.

Knead on a lightly floured surface for around 10 minutes until you have a smooth, soft round dough. Cover with a clean towel and leave to rest for 30 minutes.

Divide the dough into 4–6 palm-sized balls and roll each one into a large round, flat, thin bread.

Add 1 teaspoon salt to the spring onions and stir through. Then take the spring onion and place a handful on half of each dough circle. Fold the empty half over the spring onions to make a semi-circle and pinch the edges with a fork to seal the spring onions inside.

Turn a wok upside down (or use a large frying pan/skillet) and place on the stove over a medium heat.

Melt the butter in a separate frying pan and swirl it around until it becomes brown.

Cook the dough on the upside-down wok or frying pan for 3–4 minutes on each side. Once you finish, dip the bread into the browned butter, making sure to coat each side.

Repeat this for the other dough balls and once completed serve on a plate with a drizzle of date molasses.

کادێ

TRADITIONAL CHEESE-STUFFED BREAD

Kadê (or *zatila*) is a traditional Kurdish Jewish stuffed bread from the Badinan region, especially popular in Zakho. This flatbread is typically filled with homemade cheese and cooked on a skillet, sometimes pan-fried for a crispy crust. It can be made in various shapes, like round, half-moon or other shapes, with each family having their own style. While cheese is the traditional filling for Jewish communities in Badinan, other Kurdish regions make similar stuffed breads. In northern and eastern Kurdistan, a meat-filled version is called *shamborek* and in southern and western Kurdistan, it's filled with foraged herbs or spring onions/scallions and known as *kalana* (see page 151). No matter the filling or name, these simple, beloved breads are a staple, connecting generations through the regions.

320 g/2½ cups plain/all-purpose flour, plus extra for dusting
1 tablespoon white sugar
1 tablespoon instant dried yeast
1 teaspoon salt
200 ml/scant 1 cup warm water
2 tablespoons olive oil
200 g/7 oz. feta, crumbled
200 g/7 oz. Kurdish cheese, grated (or any other hard cheese, such as gouda)
250 ml/1 cup rapeseed oil

MAKES 6

Combine the flour, sugar and yeast in a bowl, ensuring it is well mixed, then add the salt.

Mix the warm water and olive oil together. Create a small well in the middle of the flour and slowly pour in the water and oil and mix as you go with your hands. Once it is completely combined, knead the dough for around 10 minutes until the dough is soft. Cover the dough in the bowl with a clean dish towel and place in a warm place to rise for 30 minutes.

Divide the dough into 6 portions, roll into balls and cover them while you work to prevent them drying out. Take one ball at a time, and roll it out into a thin round flatbread on a lightly floured surface.

Combine both cheeses together, then divide them between the flatbreads, placing a mound on one side of each one. Fold the other side over and use your fingers to pinch the edges shut. Flatten slightly, but don't squash it flat.

Heat the oil in a frying pan/skillet over a medium-high heat. Once hot, place the bread into the pan and fry for about 3 minutes on each side.

Serve the bread drizzled with honey for a sweet hit or as savoury bread alongside olives, fresh tomatoes and cucumber.

Nawsaji

ناوساجی

SEEDED FRIED BREAD

This thin bread is usually served with a Kurdish-style breakfast, where we have sweet black cardamom tea, plain yogurt, honey, cream cheese, walnuts and olives. This is a deep-fried bread, so some people avoid cooking this at home, because of the smell of deep-frying oil in the house. This is one of the oldest street foods. Usually women would sit outside their house with a fire pit and a deep black *manjal* (frying pan/skillet) and sell these delicious breads from their homes.

375 ml/1½ cups warm water
500 g/3½ cups strong white flour
1 teaspoon white sugar
2 teaspoons dried yeast
1½ teaspoons salt
1 tablespoon olive oil
500 ml/2 cups sunflower oil, for frying
2 tablespoons mixed black and white sesame seeds

MAKES 5–6

In a mixing bowl, put 125ml/½ cup of the warm water, 1 teaspoon of the flour, the sugar and the yeast and mix very well. Cover and let rise for 5–7 minutes.

Place the remaining flour and the salt in a bowl and slowly add the yeast mixture, the rest of the water, as well as the olive oil and mix together. Knead until you have a smooth, but slightly sticky soft dough.

Wet your hands and roll the dough into a bowl and cover with the cling film/plastic wrap, then place a clean dish towel over the top and keep in a warm place at room temperature to rise for 10 minutes.

Oil a plate very lightly, divide the dough into 5–6 balls, the size of small apples, and place them on the lightly oiled plate. Cover with cling film and let sit for about 5 minutes.

Meanwhile, put the sunflower oil in a frying pan/skillet over a medium-high heat for 3–4 minutes. To check if the oil is hot enough, put a small pinch of the dough into the hot oil and wait until the dough rises to the top and floats, that means the oil is ready.

Lightly oil the work surface to prevent the dough from sticking. Take one dough ball at a time and dip the dough into the sesame seed mixture, then place on a flat work surface and use your fingers to flatten the dough into a round disc shape. With the tips of your fingers, lightly press indentations on the surface of the dough (as if making focaccia). This will help the bread cook quickly.

With both hands, hold the bread and slide it into the hot oil, then use a fork to make small holes while it is frying. Once it's a golden colour, turn the bread and fry on the other side until very crispy. Remove from the pan and rest on paper towels to soak any excess oil. Serve with any breakfast of your choosing – sweet, savoury or both.

Drinks & sweet things

Xoshaw

خۆشاو

DRIED FRUIT DRINK & DESSERT

Xoshaw is a popular Kurdish drink. The word *xoshaw* means flavoured water, *xosh* meaning 'flavoured/nice' and *aw* meaning 'water'. It can be served as a dessert or a drink for any occasion. Feel free to add more sour fruits if you want more zingy, popping flavours in the finished drink.

Pictured on pages 156–157.

- 10 g/¼ oz. dried jumbo black grapes (*mewzh*)
- 20 g/¾ oz. dried apples
- 20 g/¾ oz. dried pears
- 25 g/1 oz. dried apricots
- 25 g/1 oz. dried figs
- 20 g/¾ oz. prunes
- 20 g/¾ oz. peaches
- 20 g/¾ oz. cranberries
- 1 cinnamon stick

TO SERVE

- 10 g/¼ oz. flaked/slivered almonds
- 15 g/½ oz. flaked/slivered pistachios
- 15 g/½ oz. chopped walnuts

SERVES 4–5

Put all the ingredients in a saucepan and add 750 ml/3 cups water. Set over a medium heat, bring to the boil and cook for 10–15 minutes. Take off the heat, cover the pan and leave overnight to soak and infuse.

To serve, scoop the fruit into a dessert cup and sprinkle with the flaked and chopped nuts. Pour the liquid into glasses and serve it cold or hot.

NOTE *This is perfect for Christmas; you can add it to red wine to make a Kurdish version of mulled wine to be enjoyed during the festive season.*

Shawchera night

One of the most beautiful aspects of Kurdish culture and tradition is always being prepared for the arrival of each season, especially winter and spring. In the long winter nights, families, neighbours and friends gather together. Every night of the month, they gather in different homes for shawchera *night. While sitting around the room, the family will start with jokes and laughter. The elderly will tell a story, or someone else will recite a poem or sing, including* Hayran *(traditional Kurdish singing without* instruments *). The* shawchera *will then be served, which includes dry or* salted *nuts like walnuts, dates, dried mulberries, dried figs and roasted seeds – sunflower seeds, pumpkin seeds, watermelon seeds, and melon seeds are all roasted and served in small bowls throughout the night.*

Desserts and hot drinks are made on the wood burner. Xoshaw *drink or dessert is part of Kurdish culture for long, cold winter nights when fresh fruit is not available. The dried fruits are placed on the wood burner, along with walnuts in their shells and* baru*, which is a type of edible acorn. Everyone enjoys the smoked nuts and drinks or eats the* xoshaw*, spending the night together, especially in neighbourhoods or villages cut off because of the snow.*

Chai raash

چای ڕەش

KURDISH BLACK TEA

Traditionally we serve this tea all day long. My mother would wake up early morning and put on the *samawer* (hot water tank), put the teapot on and keep it running until bedtime, before turning it off again. If you're very lucky to get the first tea of the day (early morning), which we call *chayi dem be kûl*, you'll enjoy the tea slowly brewed before it has gone to boiling point – the best flavour.

The most important thing is when guests arrive at your home, you serve them cold water followed by tea (alongside something sweet or savoury). Your guests will then politely indicate when they have had enough tea by laying the cup down on the saucer. This is a well-known etiquette in Kurdish culture.

This delicious tea is best served alongside any breakfast, as afternoon tea with homemade pastries (such as *kwlichay gwêz*, see page 164), or serve with savoury roasted sunflower seeds and roasted salted nuts.

2 tablespoons loose black tea leaves
600 ml/scant 2½ cups cold water
1 teaspoon rose petals
½ teaspoon rose water (optional)
sugar, to taste

heatproof enamel or metal teapot (one suitable for heating on the stove)

very small sieve/tea strainer

Middle Eastern teacup (istikan)

SERVES 4–5

Pour the water into the teapot and place on the stove over a very low heat.

Rinse the tea under cold water, add it to the teapot with the rose petals and close the lid. Let the tea brew over a very low heat for 15 minutes, without boiling.

Continue to brew until very small bubbles start to form, then set it over a tealight candle to keep brewing slowly and keep warm. Add the rose water, if using, just before serving.

Serve the tea in small clear teacups, add sugar to taste and stir until dissolved.

NOTES

- *If your tea is very strong add hot water to dilute it.*
- *Don't boil the tea let the tea brew.*
- *Mix 3-4 different tea blends together to get the flavour you want.*
- *Mix the tea with spices you like and keep in airtight containers for long lasting taste, such as cardamom, cinnamon, star anise, dried apple, rose petals and rose water.*

Dow

دۆ

YOGURT DRINK

Yogurt and water is traditionally fermented in a clay pot (*goza*) for three days with fresh herbs to achieve this refreshingly sour drink.

1 kg/2¼ lb. plain/natural yogurt
1 litre/4 cups cold water
250 ml/1 cup hot water
1 tablespoon sugar
fresh dill, chopped, to garnish
salt

SERVES 4–8

Blitz the yogurt with the cold water in a food processor or blender for 10–15 minutes until it becomes very light and fluffy. Transfer the mixture to a large airtight container, but don't fill it up to the top, leave a gap between the mixture and the lid to allow room for the gas as it ferments. Add the hot water and the sugar, stir to mix and help the fermentation process. Place the lid on the container and position it somewhere warm. and let it sit for 3 days.

After 3 days, check on it and see if it is fermented. If there are bubbles on the top and it looks a bit fizzy, that means it's done. If not, add a further 125 ml/½ cup hot water and leave it for another 3 days, then check again.

It should have a sour and fizzy taste. It's good for your gut microbiome and health. Add salt to taste as required. Serve with ice cubes and garnish with some chopped dill and a pinch of salt, mixed together before serving.

Mastaw

ماستاو

YOGURT, MINT & DILL DRINK

Mastaw has the same ingredients as Dow (see above), but it is not fermented. Add dill, salt and water and blend until it becomes lovely and frothy.

500 g/2⅓ cups Greek yogurt
15 g/½ cup chopped fresh mint (reserve some for garnishing)
15 g/½ cup fresh dill
½ tablespoon salt
juice and zest of 1 lime or lemon
100 g/½ cup crushed ice
4 slices of limes, to garnish
pickled qazwan, to decorate (optional)

SERVES 4–5

Place the yogurt, fresh herbs, salt, lime or lemon juice in a jug/pitcher with 400 ml/1⅔ cups water. Use a hand blender to blend together until the mixture is smooth and frothy – the more froth, the tastier the drink. Make sure the herbs are very smoothly blended together, and taste the mixture to see if you need to add more salt or lime juice.

To serve, divide the crushed ice between glasses and slowly pour the blended drink over the ice, not quite to the top. Use a spoon to top with some of the froth, then garnish with a slice of lime, the reserved mint and the qazwan, if using, then sprinkle over the lime zest. This is the perfect summer drink, it's also non-alcoholic, it goes very well with any kebabs/kabobs and grills and any yaprax.

NOTE *The blended mixture can be made in advance and kept in the fridge until needed, then just shaken before serving.*

Sharbati mêwzh

شەربەتی مێوژ

BLACK RAISIN DRINK

This is great to have in the summertime as a refreshing, iced and sweet drink. We would usually enjoy this during Ramadan. After the late summer when wild grapes have been harvested, they are dried to use later to create this drink. You get a delicious rich sweet flavour and, if you serve it with the raisins in the drink, you get a nice pop of rehydrated grapes as you drink it. You must serve this with crushed ice for the best flavour and it is wonderful served beside the *Berbang* (a sunset feast to celebrate breaking the daily fast during Ramadan).

500 g/1 lb. 2 oz. jumbo sun-dried raisins
½ tablespoon dried spearmint or mint (or 2 tablespoons fresh spearmint or mint)
½ beetroot/beet – use raw for best flavour and colour (optional)
juice of ½ lemon (optional)

muslin/cheesecloth

SERVES 4

Put the grapes in a saucepan, add the spearmint or mint and pour in 1.7 litres/7 cups water. Bring to the boil, then turn off the heat, cover and leave overnight to soak – this will help the grapes expand and rehydrate.

The next day, drain the grapes from the water, reserving the water for later. Place the grapes in a food processor or blender with a little of the liquid and the beetroot and lemon juice. Blitz until completely smooth.

Place the blended mixture back into a saucepan and pour the reserved water over it. Let it rest for 20 minutes so all the flavours infuse and the colour develops.

Place a piece of muslin in a sieve/strainer. Pour the drink through the sieve, squeezing the muslin until all the liquid is extracted. Pour into a jug/pitcher and place it in the fridge.

Pour into ice-filled glasses to serve.

NOTES

- *This is a sugar-free drink. If it's too sweet, you can add more water or lemon juice.*
- *If red grapes are used to make the raisins, the colour of the drink will be light red, but if the grapes are black, then the juice will be purple.*
- *You can add slices of beetroot, if preferred, this gives a distinct aroma, colour and has health benefits.*

Kwlichay gwêz

کولیچەی گوێز

SWEET WALNUT-STUFFED DUMPLINGS

Kwlichay gwêz is a popular dessert enjoyed during Jezhin (Eid). This dish is very versatile – you can use cinnamon, cardamom, rose water or orange blossom water to flavour these bite-sized dumplings. Traditionally we use cardamom and a hint of clove. Serve alongside black tea or coffee for the best flavour.

DOUGH

210 g/1½ cups plain/all-purpose flour
½ tablespoon cornflour/cornstarch
2 medium eggs
50 g/3½ tablespoons melted butter
100 g/½ cup Greek yogurt
¼ teaspoon bicarbonate of soda/ baking soda
pinch of salt
250 ml/1 cup sunflower oil

FILLING

130 g/1 cup walnuts
2 tablespoons granulated sugar
1 tablespoon ground cinnamon
pinch of ground cloves

FOR DUSTING

1 tablespoon icing/confectioners' sugar mixed with ½ teaspoon each ground cardamom and ground cinnamon

MAKES 16

Take a tablespoon of the flour and mix it with the cornflour in a small bowl and set aside.

Put the eggs, melted butter, yogurt, bicarbonate of soda and salt in a bowl and whisk together. Add the remaining flour gradually and mix to a soft dough. Bring together into a ball, cover and let rest at room temperature for 5–10 minutes.

For the filling, put the walnuts, sugar and cinnamon in a food processor and blitz until the walnuts are chopped well; not too crunchy or too fine.

Dust the work surface with the flour and cornflour mix and roll out the dough into a round, about 3 mm/⅛ inch thick.

Use a small round cookie cutter or a small glass to cut out 16 circles of dough for the dumplings. Place ½ tablespoon of the filling in the centre of each round of dough. Fold one side up over the filling and press closed with your fingers, crimping the edges as you go. Place on baking sheets until you have finished shaping all the dough.

Heat the sunflower oil in a deep frying pan/skillet over a medium-high heat until hot. To test the oil before adding the filled dough, put a pinch of the dough into the hot oil; when it starts to float, the oil is ready.

Place the dumplings in the hot oil, one by one, making sure not to overcrowd the pan. If you think that the oil is too hot, turn it down a little. Fry for 1½ minutes on each side until golden brown. Carefully remove from the pan and place on paper towels to soak up any excess oil.

Transfer to serving plates and dust with the cardamom sugar. These are best enjoyed while still warm, but are also delicious cold.

NOTES

- *This is the perfect treat for the festive season and is great for feeding to a crowd.*
- *You can alter the spices to suit your tastes – use only cardamom, or just cinnamon, or any mix you prefer.*

Shilkêna

شلكێنه

KURDISH PANCAKES

This is an old Kurdish dessert, and one that is also enjoyed as a breakfast dish. It is very rich due to the inclusion of crushed walnuts, brown butter and grape or mulberry molasses in between each layer of the pancakes. The pancakes should be large and layered like a cake, drizzled with more walnuts, brown butter and molasses and scattered with rose petals to serve. This layered dessert or breakfast can then be sliced as you would a cake to be enjoyed with family and friends. Traditionally, the pancakes are made in a large pan over an open fire.

170 g/1¼ cups plain/all-purpose flour
pinch of salt
½ teaspoon safflower powder
¼ teaspoon bicarbonate of soda/ baking soda
150 ml/⅔ cup milk
1 tablespoon Greek yogurt
½ tablespoon rose water
2 large eggs
80 g/⅓ cup/1 stick unsalted butter
50 g/2¾ oz. walnuts, chopped
3 tablespoons grape or date molasses (or butter or honey)
rose petals and sliced pistachios, to decorate

SERVES 4–6

Sift the flour, salt ,safflower and bicarbonate soda into a bowl and make a well in the middle.

Mix the milk with the yogurt, rose water, eggs and 50 ml/scant ¼ cup water and then slowly pour it into the well in the flour. Start whisking it in a little at a time until all combined and smooth.

Melt the butter in a saucepan. Remove a generous tablespoon, and set aside. Return the pan to the heat and continue to cook the butter for 5–7 minutes until it browns.

Put a pan on the stove and dry roast the chopped walnuts slightly for about 2 minutes until you can just start to smell the nutty aroma. Add the browned butter, then the molasses. Mix well, then turn the heat down. Once it starts bubbling, turn off the heat.

Put a frying pan/skillet over a medium heat. Add a teaspoon of the reserved melted butter to the pan, and add a ladleful of the pancake mixture, swirling it around to cover the base of the pan. Once it starts to turn golden and crispy, turn it over to crisp up the other side. Once cooked, remove from the pan onto a serving plate and drizzle over some of the browned butter mix (not too much) and repeat for every pancake.

Once all the pancakes are made, put the remaining butter mix over the top of the stack of pancakes and cut into wedges. Decorate with rose petals and sliced pistachios to finish.

Safflower

Tobacco farmers would often plant safflower plants among their tobacco plants if there was space. Early morning, families will go picking the tobacco and they also bring back a bundle of safflower and hang it to dry under the rashmal *(tree branches that are bound together to create shade like a natural canopy). Once dried it is used for their bread, like* Kulêra mezhga *(see page 148) and in other dishes like these pancakes.*

Galgalli

گاڵ گاڵی

SWEET BISCUIT BREAD

This is a sweet biscuit type of bread that is enjoyed alongside black cardamom tea. The name *galgalli* is an old name and most likely derives from the word *gulgulli* for 'flowers' and comes from the way that *galgalli* used to be made. Before people had ovens, this dish was made in the *tandor* at the end of the day after making bread. The women of the household would make some dough with some sweetness added to it and then they would use a *quchaka* (thimble) to press small overlapping circle shapes in the pattern of a flower on the *galgalli*. This was usually done to appease the children as it would be a bit more interesting than bread, but also not as sweet as a cake, just the perfect balance.

I remember my mum telling us that when she was young, she would make this with the neighbours in her village at the house of the person with a *tandor*. All the young girls would come together and help make *galgalli* using the *quchaka* to make the flower design. Another example of Kurdish community cooking!

1 egg
3 tablespoons white sugar
70 g/⅓ cup Greek yogurt
80 g/⅓ cup butter, melted
2 tablespoons milk powder
½ tablespoon baking powder
½ teaspoon bicarbonate of soda/baking soda
½ teaspoon ground cardamom
½ tablespoon rose water
1 teaspoon rose petal powder
½ teaspoon vanilla extract
240 g/1¾ cups plain/all-purpose flour (2 teaspoons set aside)
½ teaspoon salt
1 egg yolk
black nigella seeds, for sprinkling

FOR DUSTING

1 tablespoon icing/confectioners' sugar
1 teaspoon ground cardamom
safflower powder

SERVES 6

Preheat the oven 250°C/475°F/gas 9.

In a large bowl, whisk the egg, sugar, yoghurt, melted butter, milk powder, baking powder, bicarbonate of soda, cardamom, rose water, rose petal powder and vanilla extract to a smooth cream.

Mix the flour and salt together in a separate bowl and slowly add it to the egg mixture with your hands mixing into a nice, soft dough as you go. Cover with a clean dish towel for 5–10 minutes.

Divide the dough into 12 walnut-sized balls and shape into round cookie shapes or use any cookie cutters you like, placing them on a non-stick baking sheet as you go.

Turn the oven down to 170°C/325°F/gas 3.

Add a few drops of rose water to the egg yolk in a small bowl, beat together and then brush over the cookies. Sprinkle with black nigella seeds and bake in the oven for 15 minutes. Check if they need more time – if the outside is crispy and the bottom is browned, they are ready. Pierce the thickest area with a toothpick; if it comes out clean, they are ready.

Once baked, mix the icing sugar and cardamom together, sprinkle over the top and sprinkle with safflower powder to finish. Serve with cardamom tea or coffee.

NOTE *To make savoury biscuit bread, remove the sugar and add some crumbled cheese (like feta) and fresh parsley and serve it for breakfast.*

Miwani

میوانی

CUSTARD TOPPED WITH GOATS' CHEESE, WALNUT & PISTACHIO

Miwani is traditionally made when a woman is giving birth to a child, to help her regain her strength and energy, and symbolizes a welcoming to the baby so it goes on to have a sweet life. It is also made if someone passes away, but is made a little drier, mixed with lots of mixed nuts and made into small chunks or balls to be served alongside black tea or coffee. This symbolizes there being more sweet days after every bitterness, and celebrates the life of the person who has died. After every hard time there will be sweet times too.

1 tablespoon olive oil
1 tablespoon butter
75 g/½ cup plain/all-purpose flour
1½ tablespoons date molasses
1 tablespoon organic honey
360 ml/1½ cups water
¼ teaspoon ground cardamom
4 eggs

TO GARNISH

2 tablespoons crumbled soft goats' cheese
1 tablespoon crushed pistachios
½ teaspoon ground cinnamon mixed with 1½ tablespoons crushed walnuts

SERVES 4–5

Heat the oil in a frying pan/skillet over a medium heat, and once hot, add the butter and stir until the butter has just melted. Add the flour and keep stirring to avoid burning until all the flour has been absorbed by the butter mixture and browned.

Mix the molasses, honey and water together in a bowl. Gradually pour the molasses mixture into the browned flour, little by little. Keep stirring and keep adding the liquid until it is all finished so you get a nice smooth soft cream. Add the cardamom and keep mixing.

Turn down the heat and make a dent in the surface, add the eggs one by one. Break up the yolks with a spatula and swirl around the pan, then sprinkle a pinch of salt on the eggs and cover for 2 minutes over a low heat. It should have a soft creamy texture.

Turn off the heat, sprinkle the crumbled cheese on the top and garnish with the pistachios, cinnamon and walnuts.

Serve in the pan with any bread of your choice or cracker bread.

NOTES

- *You can drizzle over honey or molasses if you like the custard to have a sweeter taste.*
- *If you prefer a savoury version, swap the molasses with milk or water.*
- *You can make it into a sweet treat by reducing the amount of liquid and letting it cook for longer until all the liquid evaporates. You can also omit the egg and cheese and serve it plain.*
- *Mix the custard with more crushed nuts and shape into small balls to be enjoyed as a snack alongside coffee or black tea.*

Belachuk

بەلەچەک

SQUASH COOKED IN BLACK TEA & MOLASSES

During autumn the harvest of black grapes is made into vinegar, molasses or jam or sun-dried to become *mêwzh* (jumbo black raisins). Grape molasses can be used with vegetables like pumpkin, butternut squash or even fruits such as apple and pears to make compotes to be used through the winter, or used in dishes like *belachuk. Belachuk* means preserving the fruit or vegetable for longer. Traditionally this was often the main way to keep all of the harvests and not waste anything, as there were no fridges to keep fruits and vegetables fresh. The *belachuk* would be warmed up and enjoyed during the cold and often snowy evenings. The taste is fruity and sweet, made with natural sugars and is often eaten with nuts like walnuts to balance out the rich sweetness. I personally find the traditional recipe too sweet so I include black tea to add some bitterness and a deeper brown colour and serve it with ice cream (preferably tahini flavour) to add a creamy nuttiness.

- 200 g/7 oz. sieved ash (from charcoal or burnt wood)
- 1 butternut squash, peeled, deseeded, halved and cut into half moons
- 2 tablespoons black tea leaves (I use cardamom)
- 500 ml/2 cups hot water
- 100 g/½ cup granulated sugar
- 100 g/3½ oz. date/grape molasses
- 1 tablespoon freshly squeezed lemon juice
- ice cream, to serve

HONEY-GLAZED WALNUTS

- 100 g/¾ cup walnuts
- 1½ tablespoons runny honey

muslin/cheesecloth

SERVES 4

Mix the ash with 1 litre/4 cups water and set aside to set for 1½–2 hours.

Place the muslin inside a sieve/strainer set over a large bowl and pour the ash water through the sieve to remove the ash, discarding the solids. Put the butternut squash in the ash water and leave to soak for at least 1½ hours to cure.

Brew the tea in the hot water for 3–5 minutes, then strain.

While the butternut squash is curing, pour 2 litres/8 cups water into a saucepan and add the sugar, molasses, lemon juice and strained tea and bring to the boil.

Take the squash out of the ash water, wash and rinse well with cold water. Add to the molasses mixture and cook for at least 1 hour until the squash is crispy on the outside, but soft inside, and the sauce is reduced to half.

To make the honey-glazed walnuts, fry the walnuts in a frying pan/skillet until they brown and you can smell the roasting nuts. Add the honey and toss the nuts so that they are well coated without burning. Quickly remove from the heat, tip onto a baking sheet and spread out to avoid the nuts sticking together.

Serve the *belachuk* cold with your favourite ice cream on the side and garnish with the honey-glazed walnuts to finish.

NOTE *You can make this in a big batch and keep it in an airtight jar or container in the fridge. Use it within 3 weeks.*

Index

Acknowledgements

It's not always easy to find the right words to thank the people who have stood by you, inspired you, and believed in you, especially on a journey as personal and meaningful as this one.

This book is more than just a collection of recipes. It is a reflection of my life, my culture, and the people who have shaped both. From cooking with my aunties, to establishing the restaurant in London and now, to the pages of this book, what an incredible journey it has been.

Along the way, I've met some truly wonderful people who believed in me, encouraged me and helped bring this dream to life.

First and foremost, my deepest thanks to my publisher, Ryland Peters and Small, and the truly lovely team who made this book possible: Leslie, Abi, Julia, Megan, Kathy, Clare, and the entire prop and styling team. Your hard work, care and creativity shine on every page.

A heartfelt thank you to Amal Khalidi, my assistant, who has been by my side throughout this entire journey. I will always cherish the time we spent together creating this book. Your dedication and support mean the world to me.

To my family, my husband and my sons, thank you for your endless love, patience and support. You've worked hard beside me for years, and your belief in me has been my strength. I am so grateful to have you in my life.

And to my divided homeland, Kurdistan, thank you for giving me this rich, beautiful culture. You have inspired every word, every dish and every memory in these pages. We may live far from each other, but as the Kurdish saying goes, '2 + 2 doesn't make four, it becomes one.' No matter where we are, we carry you in our hearts.

Our cuisine, like our music, dance, language and heritage, has always been passed down from generation to generation, untouched and unchanged. This book is a tribute to that legacy, to the way our great-great-grandmothers cooked, and to the traditions that have lived on through time. In writing this book, I discovered so much more about my own culture and found a renewed perspective on what it means to be Kurdish. I hope, in reading it, you will too.

Thank you from the bottom of my heart.